The Baseball Life
of Willie Mays

by Lee Greene

Illustrated with photographs

Cover photograph of Willie Mays
by Martin Blumenthal
for *Sport* Magazine

SCHOLASTIC BOOK SERVICES

NEW YORK • TORONTO • LONDON • AUCKLAND • SYDNEY • TOKYO

Copyright © 1972, 1970 by Lee Greene. All rights reserved. Pub-lished by Scholastic Book Services, a division of Scholastic Magazines, Inc.

6th printing .... September 1972

Printed in the U.S.A.

CONTENTS

1. "The Greatest Player"   5

2. Growing Up in Alabama   14

3. From the Black Barons to the Giants   26

4. "Tell Durocher I'm Not Coming"   37

5. Rookie Center Fielder of the Giants   50

6. Bring on the Yankees   66

7. Private Willie Mays   72

8. Return to Glory   83

9. Star of the Series   95

10. Good-by, New York   105

11. Hello, San Francisco   113

12. Hero of Candlestick Park at Last   129

13. "He Can Still Do It All"   144

Appendix:
   Willie Mays' Record   159

Willie Mays

1

"The Greatest Player"

THE smile spread over Willie Mays' face and he started to laugh. It was a high, squeaking laugh that echoed through the clubhouse of the old Polo Grounds in New York.

"Say hey," he said to the sportswriter, when he was able to stop laughing. "You've got to be kidding me. Ask me that question again."

"I'm not kidding, Willie," said the sportswriter. "I just asked if you expected to win the batting title, the Most Valuable Player award, or both."

Willie Mays started to laugh again. But when he saw that the sportswriter was really serious, Willie stopped laughing. He thought for a moment and then answered slowly: "The batting title and the Most Valuable Player award are two of the greatest things a ballplayer can have. I don't expect to win either one of them. I've never won anything like that in my life. But if I can help the Giants win another pennant, I'll be a happy man."

It was September of 1954, and the New York Giants held a narrow lead over the powerful Brooklyn Dodgers in the closing weeks of an exciting pennant race. Just as exciting as this battle between the two rival teams was the hitting duel between their batting stars. Both the Dodgers' Duke Snider and the Giants' Willie Mays were having excellent seasons, with batting averages around .340. A favorite argument around New York City was, which man was the better hitter. Snider had led for most of the year. But in September — the day the Giants finally clinched the pennant with a victory over the Dodgers — Willie got three hits to raise his average to .344. That took the lead away from Snider.

But there was still a week left of the 1954 season, and the Giants' manager, Leo Durocher, had a very unusual problem. Now that the Giants had won the pennant, he planned to rest Willie Mays and some of the other players so that they would be fresh and ready for the World Series. Durocher felt the rest would also help Willie's chances of keeping his lead in the competition for the batting championship.

If the race had been just between Mays and Snider, Durocher would have gone ahead with his plan to rest Willie. Now, however, a new contender appeared. It was Don Mueller, the right fielder who played alongside center fielder Willie Mays in the New York Giants' outfield.

"What a spot I'm in," Durocher complained to newsmen. "I'd love to take Mays out of the line-up for a few days, but with Mueller in the race I can't play favorites. They both have to go all the way."

There never has been a closer race than the one these three fine hitters waged in the final days of the 1954 season. This is how they stood as they prepared to play the final game on September 26th:

MUELLER	.3426
SNIDER	.3425
MAYS	.3422

For that final game the Giants went to Philadelphia to play the Phillies. The opposing pitcher was Robin Roberts, an outstanding right-hander who had won twenty-three games that season. At the same time, Duke

Manager Leo Durocher cheers as Willie Mays rounds third. Mays' homer really counted in the close 1954 pennant race against the Brooklyn Dodgers.

Snider and the Dodgers were going against a much weaker Pittsburgh Pirates' team and a rookie pitcher named Jake Thies.

Some of the Giant players were angry when they learned that the Pirates were not starting one of their good pitchers against the Dodgers. The odds, the Giants felt, were strongly loaded in Snider's favor.

"It's not fair to Willie and Don," said one of them. "They have to hit against one of the best pitchers in the league, while Snider goes against a nobody."

Willie just grinned when he heard that. "You don't hear Don or me complaining, do you?" he said. "Heck, if we can't hit the best, we don't deserve to win the batting title."

As the Giants prepared to bat in the top of the first inning, Mueller was listed as the third man in the batting order, and Mays was listed fifth. In his first time at bat, Mueller rapped a clean single. In the Giants' dugout Willie Mays was one of the first to shout his congratulations.

"Nice going, Don!" his high-pitched voice shouted across the infield.

Moments later, Willie also hit a hard single in his first time at bat. The race was still going strong. Then Mueller fouled out in his next time at bat, and Mays matched him by grounding out. Mueller had flied out in his third time at bat when Willie came up in the seventh inning. The Phillies' center fielder, Richie Ashburn, moved a few steps toward left field as he always did when Mays was at bat. This made sense because Willie usually hit the ball to the left side of the field. But not this time.

Timing a Robin Roberts' fast ball perfectly, Willie drove the ball far enough to the right of Ashburn so that neither he nor the right fielder, Del Ennis, could reach it. The ball rolled to the outfield wall as Willie streaked around the bases with a triple.

"Bet you can't do that again, Willie," one of his teammates teased when the inning was over. Willie grinned and said, "You just watch me. It's going to cost you a Coke."

Sure enough, in the very next inning, after Mueller had flied out again, Willie stroked another ball into almost the same spot. This time, Ashburn was able to pick up the ball more quickly and stop Willie at second base. While he was standing there, Willie looked toward the Giants' dugout and made a drinking motion. The Coke was in the bag.

The score was tied at 2–2 when Mueller

came to bat in the tenth inning and got his second hit, a double. He was still standing on second base when Willie came to bat. Even the Philadelphia fans were shouting now for Willie to get his fourth hit of the day. But Roberts never gave him that chance. He figured that Mays was too dangerous in a situation where a single would score the winning run. So, with no one on first base, he walked Willie intentionally in order to pitch to another batter.

Before Willie could come to bat again, the Giants managed to score the winning run. But the single, double, and triple that he had hit under such great pressure were enough to win the batting championship. (Mueller had gotten only two hits, and Snider had gone hitless in Pittsburgh.) These were the final standings:

MAYS	.345
MUELLER	.342
SNIDER	.341

In the dressing room, the other Giants pounded and thumped Willie on the back. He grinned back, accepting their congratulations. But when things quieted down, he went over to Mueller's locker.

11

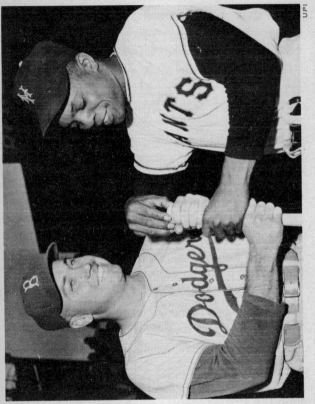

Duke Snider and Willie Mays fool around before a 1954 night game.
These two star center fielders were strong rivals for the batting championship.

"You deserved to win it, Don," he said.

The disappointed Mueller smiled and answered, "Don't give me that, Willie. Any time you can get three clutch hits off Roberts in one game, you ought to be the champ. I'm just glad the title went to a Giant."

The next afternoon, millions of New Yorkers cheered the Giants in a ticker-tape parade down Broadway. At City Hall, where the team was greeted by the mayor, Leo Durocher introduced each player. As Willie stepped forward, Durocher shouted into the microphone, "And now, ladies and gentlemen, here is the greatest player I have ever laid eyes on — Willie Mays!" The applause was deafening as thousands of voices shouted their approval.

A few days later, Willie Mays and the New York Giants astounded the baseball world by winning four straight games from the favored Cleveland Indians in the World Series. Not long afterward, Willie Mays was named the National League's Most Valuable Player for 1954.

In the same year he had won two of the most cherished prizes a ballplayer could win. "I don't expect to win either one of them," he had said. But he had won them both.

2

Growing Up in Alabama

WILLIE HOWARD MAYS' first toy was a great big ball that Willie's father gave him on his first birthday. Willie couldn't walk yet, but he loved to play with that ball. When his father rolled it to him, Willie would grab it and try to throw it back. If no one was around to play with him, Willie would bounce the ball, or roll it around the room and crawl after it.

As he got older, his father brought home other balls. There were basketballs, footballs, and, especially, baseballs for Willie's father was a fine baseball player, just as Willie's grandfather had been before him. Some of Willie's happiest days were spent watching his father play on the semiprofessional teams around Fairfield, Alabama, where Willie grew up. Sometimes Willie would sit with his father and the other players on the bench. His greatest thrill would come when his father, playing in the outfield, made a long run to catch a ball that might have been a base hit.

"Nice going, Kitty Kat!" the other players would shout and Willie would jump up and down with excitement, knowing they were using their favorite nickname for his father.

They had a nickname for Willie, too. Someone noticed that Willie had an odd way of running, with his feet flat on the ground. In a joking way he said that Willie ran like a duck. So they called him "Buckduck" for a while. Later it was shortened to just plain "Buck," and that is what Willie Mays is still called today by his old friends.

Growing up in Fairfield in the 1930's was fun for Willie. He lived with his Aunt Sarah in her pleasant home. Willie's parents had been divorced when he was still a baby, so he never got to know his mother very well. But his Aunt Sarah treated Willie like one of her own children.

Though his father didn't live in the same house, Mr. Mays stopped by every day on his way home from the steel mill where he worked. Willie always looked forward to his visits, and the chance that his father might take him along to a baseball game if he was playing that afternoon.

If there was no game that day, Willie and his father would cross the street to a big vacant lot where the neighborhood children played. The boy would pull on a battered old glove and catch baseballs batted to him by his father. Sometimes the balls were hit on the ground, and sometimes they were hit in the air. Often his father would hit the ball over the boy's head or off to one side to see how fast Willie could chase the ball. The boy caught most of them, and when he made a very difficult catch, his high-pitched laugh echoed around the vacant lot. Willie's father was secretly very proud of the way his son could catch, but he tried not to show it.

"It's those big hands of yours," he would say. "Why, with hands that big, you should never drop a ball."

When his father was at work during the day, Willie would go out to the vacant lot with his best friend, Charley Willis. If there weren't enough other boys around to play a game, Willie and Charley would take turns throwing a baseball as high in the air as they could. The other boy would try to catch it. Willie would always win even when Charley threw the ball over his head. Willie would simply turn and run at full speed to where the ball was about to drop. He made it look easy. If Charley threw the ball so that it would land in front of Willie, Willie would come charging in and catch the ball beside his hip. After a while, Charley refused to play that game with Willie. In fact, by the time Willie was eight years old, he had to play ball with boys three or four years older than himself. He was just too good for those of his own age.

Every boy has a major-league baseball hero, and Willie's hero was Joe DiMaggio of the New York Yankees. In 1941, when the boy was only ten years old, DiMaggio set a baseball record by hitting in fifty-six straight games. During the last few weeks of that amazing streak, Willie sat crouched in front of the radio, holding his breath, waiting to hear if DiMaggio had gotten his hit that day.

By the time the streak finally ended, Willie was determined to follow in the footsteps of his idol. He had seen DiMaggio in newsreels at the local movie theater, and he practiced the long running strides, the wide batting stance, and the smooth, flat swing of the great major leaguer.

Up to that time, Willie had played a number of positions in the neighborhood games. He even liked to pitch occasionally. But now he announced to his friends that his regular position would be in center field — Joe DiMaggio's position.

When Willie was older, he begged his father to take him to Birmingham to see the professional ball games. Sometimes they watched the white players of the Birmingham Barons in the Southern Association. At other times they would see the Birmingham Black Barons, an all-Negro team that played only other all-Negro teams. There were two teams with the same name in Birmingham, one for white players and one for blacks. Negroes couldn't play in the regular professional baseball leagues, so they had teams of their own.

Willie made up his mind that if he couldn't play center field for the New York Yankees some day, he would play for the Black Barons.

Willie continued to perfect his baseball skills. Because there was no Little League in Fairfield in those years, he spent more and more time working out with older boys. Many of them played semiprofessional baseball, like his father, and it wasn't long before Willie found himself being used occasionally as a pinch-hitter or as a substitute outfielder in some of their games. The boy was big for his age; he was only sixteen years old when he became a regular center fielder on his father's team.

Semiprofessional baseball was a lot of fun. The games were usually played in late afternoon to avoid the mid-day heat. It was the custom in the late innings of each game to "pass the hat" among the spectators. Most people threw in a few coins, and once in a while a dollar bill. Then the money was evenly divided among the members of both teams. At first Willie wouldn't take any money. After all, he was just a boy and many of the other players were grown men. But his father felt that Willie contributed as much as any man on the team. He insisted that his son accept a full share, even if it was only a dollar or two. The few dollars he earned made Willie realize that some day he might be able to make a living playing the game he loved.

Making a living was something Willie didn't like to think about as a teen-ager. In time he might have taken a job in the steel mill, but his father wouldn't hear of it.

"There's no future for you in the mill," his father said. "I wouldn't be working there myself if I hadn't married very young and had to support a family. Now it's too late for me to get out, but I want something better for you, Willie."

Willie enrolled at Fairfield Industrial High School and studied to be a clothing presser. But he hated the press machine, and he hated doing homework when he could hear his friends playing ball across the street.

What Willie liked best in high school was sports. Fairfield Industrial had no baseball team, but it did offer football and basketball. Willie soon became a star player in both sports. The football coach didn't often find a player like Willie Mays. As a high school freshman, Willie could run faster and throw a football better than any other player on the team. The coach made him a halfback in the starting line-up, and Willie worked hard. He played almost every minute of every game, but most of the other teams were stronger than Fairfield Industrial and usually won.

Willie was happier playing basketball in the winter. He wasn't as tall as some of the other players, but he was a good shooter. In his first season, he led all the other high school players in the county in scoring, and helped Fairfield Industrial to one of its best basketball records. Willie Mays was consid-

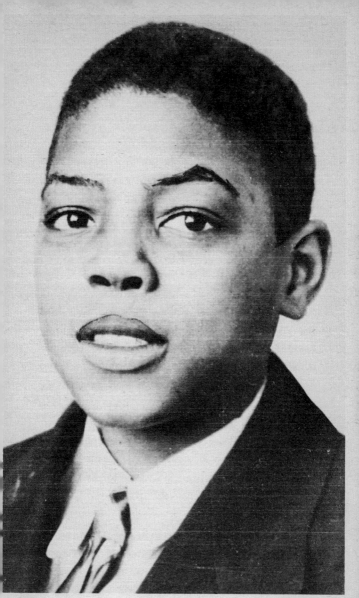

UPI

Willie as a young teenager. He was big for his age, so the older boys would sometimes let him play in their games.

ered the outstanding athlete in the school, and his classmates were proud of him. Even the teachers admired Willie, and some of them encouraged him to go on to college on an athletic scholarship.

"There are some colleges up North that give scholarships to Negro boys who are good football players," one of the teachers told Willie. "If you work a little harder in class and get better grades, you might win one of those scholarships."

The idea of going to college in the North fascinated Willie. He had never been out of Alabama, and he wondered what it was like up North. Sometimes he daydreamed about walking across a pretty campus like the ones he saw in the movies, wearing a college football sweater. But it was only a daydream. Willie didn't really want to leave home. He made up his mind to graduate from Fairfield Industrial, take a job as a presser in a local laundry, and try to earn some money on the side playing semiprofessional baseball. As things turned out, Willie didn't do any of these things.

One afternoon in the spring of 1948, when Willie was finishing his second year of high school, his father came to Aunt Sarah's house. Willie could tell that he was excited.

"Willie," his father blurted out, "how would you like to play for the Black Barons this summer?"

Willie was speechless! He had often seen the Black Barons play and knew they were one of the best Negro baseball teams in the South. Did they really want a kid like him?

"They're having tryouts," his father continued. "I know you can make that team. And, what's more, Piper Davis agrees with me."

Piper Davis was the manager of the Black Barons; he sometimes signed semiprofessional players from the Birmingham area. But Willie had never heard of any sixteen-year-old players on the Black Barons.

"Don't you think I'm a little too young for them?" Willie asked. "After all, I still have two years of high school left."

"It's true," his father said. "You know how often I've told you to finish school and learn a trade. But things are different now."

"What things?" asked Willie.

"I'll tell you what's different," his father said. "You've got a chance now to play in the big leagues, just like your Joe DiMaggio. Ever since Jackie Robinson made good with the Brooklyn Dodgers last year, and showed the world that a Negro boy can play big-league baseball, the teams are all looking for good Negro players. Piper Davis tells me that he keeps getting calls from big-league scouts, and he says they are making up lists of the best Negro players. Some of them have already been offered contracts."

Playing in the big leagues! That had always been Willie's favorite dream. But it had always seemed impossible. Now he could feel the excitement growing inside him. He really *did* have a chance to play in the major leagues — if he could make good with the Black Barons.

"Does Mr. Davis really think I can make good?" he asked eagerly.

"Sure he does," his father answered, smiling. "Oh, he thinks you've got a lot to learn. He told me you're too small for that big Di-Maggio stance, and that you could hit a curve ball better. But I told him he could teach you those things. Well, are you interested?"

"Sure I'm interested," Willie answered. "But if I'm a professional baseball player, can I still play football and basketball for my high school?"

"I'm afraid not," his father said. "You won't be eligible to play high school sports any more."

That was a blow to Willie. He knew the

football and basketball teams needed him, and that his classmates were counting on him. For a moment he hesitated. But then that old dream of playing in the major leagues came back to him, stronger than ever.

"You tell Mr. Davis I'm going to try out for his team," he said. "And you can also tell him that I'm going to make his team."

Willie's father smiled. "That's what I hoped you'd say," he answered.

The carefree days of Willie's Alabama boyhood were over, and Willie Mays' baseball career was about to begin.

3

From the Black Barons to the Giants

"COME on, Buck," yelled Piper Davis. "Get your feet closer together and don't crowd the plate so much. Your name is Willie Mays, not Joe DiMaggio."

Willie nodded his head and changed his batting stance as the Black Barons' manager had ordered.

"Don't throw him anything but curve balls," Davis shouted to the batting-practice pitcher. "He's got to learn to hit them."

Grimly, Willie gripped his bat and waited for the pitch. Sure enough, another curve ball. Willie swung and hit it, but not very hard. He shook his head and mumbled to himself. Like most good hitters, he liked to hit fast balls. But Davis had quickly spotted Willie's weakness against curve balls, and he had Willie working hard to correct it.

"Learn to take a short, quick swing instead of a big, slow one," the manager advised him. Willie did as he was told, and by the time the Black Barons were ready to begin the 1948 season, he was not only a member of the team but he was hitting the curve ball consistently.

Playing for a team like the Black Barons was a brand-new experience for a youngster who had never played anything harder than semiprofessional baseball. The team traveled around the country by bus, and Willie had to learn how to sleep on a hard bus seat during overnight trips to cities like St. Louis, Cleveland, and New York. Being away from home was also hard on Willie because he missed his father, his friends, and Aunt Sarah's cooking.

But it was a thrill to see cities that had always seemed so far away. The Black Barons played many of their games on major-league baseball fields in the big cities. One of these fields was the Polo Grounds in New York, the home field of the Giants. The field was longer and narrower than most baseball parks, so it had a very deep center field, and very short foul lines. For Willie, the shape was just perfect. As a center fielder, he had all the space he needed to chase and catch long drives that would have been home runs in other parks. As a hitter, he found it fairly simple to drive the ball down the left-field foul line for a home run. The Polo Grounds became one of his favorite parks.

Willie played very well in his first season as a professional. He batted over .300 and was very proud of one hit — a single he got while batting against Satchel Paige, the greatest pitcher in the Negro leagues.

"How about that," Piper Davis said to him after the game. "Why, there are oldtimers I know who have been trying for years to get a hit off Paige. And this fresh kid does it the first time up."

Willie just smiled and looked embarrassed.

It was also during the first season that Willie got to see his first major-league game. The Black Barons, who were scheduled to play a night game in St. Louis, arrived in the city early one afternoon and Willie had a chance to go out to the ball park and watch the old St. Louis Browns play the Boston Red Sox. It was the first time that Willie had ever seen Ted Williams, the great Red Sox hitter, and he was amazed at how fast and hard Williams could swing a bat.

Sometimes Willie wondered if he had done the right thing in becoming a professional

UPI

An artist's view of Willie Mays at seventeen, when he played professional ball with the Birmingham Black Barons.

baseball player. There were hard days when he had to play baseball after staying awake all night on the bouncing bus. And he certainly wasn't getting rich playing with the Black Barons. The Negro teams didn't pay their players very much money; Willie's salary was $75 a month. But he still dreamed of playing for a major-league team some day, and he found himself running and swinging a little faster when he knew there was a major-league scout in the stands.

And the scouts did come to see the Black Barons play. But none of them talked to Willie.

When the Black Barons' 1948 season ended, Willie kept right on playing baseball with the barnstormers. Barnstormers were informal baseball teams that traveled around the country, playing games wherever they could make a few dollars. The teams were a mixture of old and young players, and the men could play any position they felt like playing. Willie was delighted with the easy-going atmosphere so much like the old sandlot days in Fairfield.

Willie joined a barnstorming team organized by Roy Campanella, an outstanding catcher who had become the second Negro player to join the Brooklyn Dodgers. Campanella, a good-natured and kindly man, brought out the playful side of young Willie Mays. For example, there was the day in New Orleans that Campanella's team found itself without a shortstop.

"I need a volunteer," Campanella told his players. "Has anybody here ever played shortstop?"

Willie's eyes twinkled with mischief as he answered, "I'm your boy, Campy. I may play the outfield, but I'm really a fine shortstop. Why, that's my best position!"

Campanella was doubtful, but he had no choice. So, for the first and only time in his professional career, Willie Mays started a game at shortstop. He threw his body in front of the first ball that was hit his way, then got up, and somehow made the throw to first base. The next time, he misplayed a bouncing ball that almost hit him in the face. Campanella immediately signaled for time.

"I'm making a line-up change," he told the umpire. "My shortstop and center fielder are changing places."

After the inning, Willie went over to Campanella. "Why didn't you leave me in at shortstop?" he asked with a straight face. "I was just getting warmed up."

"A guy can get the electric chair for murder in this state," Campanella replied with a grin. "If I left you in at shortstop, I would have been guilty of murder."

Willie's high-pitched laugh rang out.

For two years — 1948 and 1949 — Willie played baseball almost all year long with the Black Barons and barnstorming teams. He worked hard on every part of his game, his hitting, fielding, and base running, and he knew from the way the other players talked about him that he was good enough to play in the major leagues. Still, no scout approached him and he felt badly about it.

Actually, unknown to Willie, some of the scouts *had* noticed him and had sent favorable reports on his ability to their teams. But each of the reports noted Willie's age and the fact that he was not yet a high school graduate. Baseball regulations forbid the signing of a player until his high school class has been graduated. In Willie's case that would not be until June of 1950.

When 1950 rolled around, and Willie had started his third season with the Black Barons, he finally got a chance to talk to a major-league scout — one who had not seen Willie in his two earlier seasons with the Black Barons. In a way, the discovery of Willie Mays was accidental.

Early in 1950 the Black Barons had played a game at the Polo Grounds in New York. One of the spectators was an executive of the New York Giants named Jack Schwarz. It was his job to supply players for the Giants' minor-league teams, and he thought he might find a player or two on the Black Barons that he could use. He did spot one player he liked. But it was first baseman Alonzo Perry, and not center fielder Willie Mays.

When Schwarz got back to his office and looked at the reports sent in by the Giants' scouts, he found no mention of Perry. So he called Eddie Montague, who scouted the Birmingham area for the Giants, and asked him to take a look at Perry when the Black Barons returned home. A few days later, Montague was in the stands when the Black Barons played a double-header.

At first Montague watched Perry and made notes on the first baseman's hitting and fielding. But before long his attention began to stray to another Black Baron player. It was a slim youngster with a fast and powerful swing, tremendous speed, a spectacular fielding style, and a great throwing arm. Montague checked his program and found the youngster's name. It was Willie Mays.

The more Montague watched Mays, the more excited he became. Later he would write that "this was the greatest young ballplayer I had ever seen in my life."

When the double-header was over, Montague hurried to the Black Barons' dressing room. He got there as Willie was returning from the shower, and the scout was immediately impressed by the young athlete's build. Montague had been concerned about Willie's size — the fact that he was quite slim and weighed less than 170 pounds. But one look at Willie's solid, muscular body convinced the scout that the slimness was nothing to worry about.

Montague chatted with Willie for a few minutes, asking him about himself and discussing the game with him. But the scout gave no hint that he was especially interested in Willie. When he left the dressing room, though, Montague felt strongly that he had made a real "find."

As soon as he could, Montague called New York. He told Schwarz that Alonzo Perry was not major-league material, but that the Black Barons had a nineteen-year-old center fielder who couldn't miss. Then he read off his notes on Willie Mays.

"If he's that good, go get him," said Schwarz.

The next day the Black Barons were playing a game in Tuscaloosa, Alabama. One of the first people to arrive at the field was Eddie Montague. He immediately took Willie aside and asked him if he would like to play baseball for the New York Giants.

Willie's big smile spread all over his face. "Yes, sir!" he answered quietly.

"Good," said Montague. "I'll get in touch with the team owner and see about buying your contract."

"What contract?" replied Willie. "I never signed a contract with the Barons. If you want me to play for the Giants, you'll have to deal with me directly." He gave Montague his address and telephone number, and Montague promised to call him the next day.

After their talk, Montague went into the stands to watch the game. It was obvious that Willie was in top form. He was hitting hard line drives in all directions. Late in the game he made a great catch after a long run and got off a perfect throw without even stopping to brace himself. Montague could hardly wait to get Willie's name on a Giants' contract.

He got it the next afternoon, in the living

room of Aunt Sarah's house. Willie, his father, and Aunt Sarah listened carefully while Montague explained the terms of the contract. Willie was to get a bonus of $5,000 for signing, then he would report to the Giants' farm team at Trenton, New Jersey. The scout explained that it usually took about three years in the minor leagues before a player was ready for the major leagues, but in Willie's case, he said, it might take only a year or two. When he finished, Willie put his name at the bottom of the contract. Because he was still a minor, his father also signed.

Willie watched the scout head for his car with the signed contract in his pocket. "Well, I did it," said Willie.

"It's not the New York Yankees," his father said, teasing him.

Willie laughed. "No, but it's awful close. And I like the idea of playing for the Giants. The Polo Grounds is a wonderful park for me, and I've gotten to know some people up in Harlem, only a few minutes away from the park. I think I'm going to like it there."

But first, Willie Mays had to prove himself in the minor leagues. The first stop was Trenton, New Jersey.

4

"Tell Durocher
I'm Not Coming"

TRENTON was a new world for Willie Mays. Actually he had resented being sent there because it was so far down the minor-league ladder — the Class B Interstate League. Willie figured that the Black Barons were at least the equivalent of Class AAA — the very best of the minor-league classifications. Trenton seemed like a demotion to him. The players were mostly kids, not much older than he was, with fewer skills and far less experience.

Against such easy competition, Willie would soon become a hitting terror. In 81 games for Trenton in that 1950 season, he was to belt out 108 hits — including 32 for extra bases — for a batting average of .353. Yet Willie's feelings, as he headed toward Trenton to begin training, could be summed up in one word: terror.

At Trenton, for the first time in his life, Willie Mays would be playing with white teammates under the direction of a white manager, and he was scared. He had heard stories about Negro players not being permitted to eat in the same restaurants and live in the same hotels as their white teammates. He'd heard how some white players went out of their way to be nasty and sarcastic to Negro players, or ignore the Negro players and act as if they didn't exist. On the train from Birmingham to Trenton, Willie thought about all these things. He was ready for the worst by the time he finished the long ride.

But right from the start, Trenton manager Chick Genovese and general manager Bill McKechnie, Jr., tried to put Willie at ease. They told him he was starting in center field immediately. Willie was grateful for that, but his first days in a Trenton uniform were hardly anything to celebrate. In his first twenty-two times at bat, Willie failed to get a hit.

"How am I going to hit this pitching?" he asked McKechnie. "What am I doing wrong?"

"You're not doing anything wrong," answered McKechnie. "The main thing is not

38

to worry. Just go up there and take your swings."

The answer gave Willie exactly the bit of confidence he needed. Finally he got his first hit in the next game and he didn't stop hitting for the rest of the season.

Confidence came in other ways, too. It was obvious, after the first few days, that the white players on the team were not only talking to Willie, but they genuinely liked him. In fact, it would have been hard not to like Willie Mays. When things were going right, as they usually were, Willie's high-pitched laugh filled the dressing room, and his big grin made everyone feel good. Before long, the players had even picked up Willie's favorite expression, "Say hey." It was Willie's way of calling out to a player when he couldn't remember his name.

Other forms of discrimination that Willie had known about failed to appear. He ate with his teammates, used the same rest rooms, and sat where he pleased on the team bus. There was no problem with hotels because the teams didn't use them. When the players weren't sleeping on the bus, they stayed at local YMCAs or inexpensive boarding houses. The sleeping wasn't very comfortable a lot of the time, but it was never segregated.

But the Giants hadn't sent Willie to Trenton just to break him in gently. He was also there to learn about a side of baseball that he had never thought much about before — strategy. Willie had always depended on his great natural skills and instincts, and at first he was baffled by the short baseball "quizzes" conducted by Genovese and McKechnie.

"Tie score, two out," one of them would bark. "The other team has a man on second base, a pinch-hitter up, and the pitcher on deck. How do you play it?"

"That's the manager's problem," Willie complained. "I'm not a manager."

"But you might be some day, Willie," said McKechnie. "And even if you aren't, you'll be a better baseball player if you understand the whole game, not just your part of it. Now take some of the questions we ask you about pitching. We know you're not a pitcher. But if you understand how a pitcher thinks, it will help you to become a better hitter."

Willie began to understand what it was all about, then. The bothersome quizzes took on new importance, and he began to appreciate the pointers that Genovese gave him. For example, there was the time that Willie grumbled to the manager that he didn't seem to be getting many home runs. That season he had hit only four.

The manager laughed and said, "It doesn't matter if you don't hit many home runs as long as you drive in the runs. The important thing is that those other guys *think* you might hit a home run every time you come to bat. That's why they play so deep for you. With a setup like that, you can get all the singles and doubles you want."

The explanation not only made sense to Willie, but it made him think about the way he himself played the outfield. Now he began to experiment to see just how close he could play without hurting his ability to get back quickly. He learned to gauge not only the hitter, the situation, and the pitcher, but the condition of the ground — whether it was soft or hard, wet or dry. Willie Mays was a good outfielder when he reported to Trenton. By the time he left, he was a superb one.

The reports that flowed from Trenton to the Giants' headquarters in New York were impressive. Willie Mays was everything that Eddie Montague had said he was — and maybe even more. An interested reader of those reports was a man Willie Mays had

41

never met — a man who would soon play a dominant role in his life: Leo Durocher.

Durocher was a fiery little manager who had established his reputation by molding the Brooklyn Dodgers from the National League doormat into a powerhouse. Two years earlier, in the mid-season of 1948, the baseball world had been shocked when Durocher shifted from the Dodgers to their arch rivals, the Giants. Now he was trying to do for the Giants what he had done for the Dodgers.

Durocher had inherited a team that boasted powerful hitting, but lacked speed, good pitching, and, most important of all, the desire to win. For Durocher, a man who hated to lose, this was the worst fault of all.

The Giants hadn't won a pennant since 1937. With Durocher in 1948 and 1949, they had improved a little and finished in fifth place. Then Durocher decided it was time to make some drastic changes. He made up his mind to put together a new kind of Giant team, one that would bunt and steal and run and fight hard for every run.

As early as 1949, he began to get rid of his big, slow sluggers. They weren't the scrappy, aggressive kind of player that Durocher wanted. First, he traded one of the team's biggest power hitters, catcher Walker Cooper, to Cincinnati. Then he brought up from the minor leagues three players who met his qualifications: catcher Wes Westrum, infielder Hank Thompson, and outfielder Monte Irvin. Thompson and Irvin were the first Negroes to play for the Giants and both were quickly assigned to starting positions. Before the season was over, Durocher had sold another of his old sluggers, Johnny Mize, to the Yankees. When the season ended, Willard Marshall, Johnny Kerr, and Sid Gordon were shipped to the Boston Braves in return for shortstop Alvin Dark and second baseman Eddie Stanky.

The new-style Giants began to excite the New York fans in 1950. For the first time in years the team was a pennant contender, and finished a strong third behind the Philadelphia Phillies and the Dodgers. Durocher had put together a fine pitching staff with starters like Sal Maglie, Larry Jansen, and Jim Hearn. Westrum had taken over the catching chores; Stanky and Dark performed brilliantly around second base; and both Thompson and Irvin enjoyed excellent seasons.

Many baseball writers were so impressed by the Giants' fast finish in 1950 that they predicted a New York pennant in 1951. Durocher himself was confident that his reorganized team could finish first without adding any new players. But he was impressed by the progress reports on the youngster named Willie Mays, so he approved his promotion to the Giants' top farm team at Minneapolis for 1951. Then Durocher made a mental note to take a look at this new prospect as soon as he could.

For Willie, the experience of his first spring training camp worked out well. At Sanford, Florida, where both the Giants and their farm teams trained together, Willie found himself readily accepted by his new manager, Tommy Heath, and his new teammates. One day he was called aside to meet a couple of interested visitors, Horace Stoneham, the Giants' owner, and Leo Durocher.

The first meeting of Mays and Durocher was brief. The two men looked at each other and liked what they saw. They chatted for a moment and Durocher said, "We got quite a report on you from Trenton."

"Oh yeah?" replied Willie. "What did it say?"

"It said your hat keeps flying off whenever you catch a fly ball," answered Durocher, and they both laughed.

Then they shook hands and Durocher said, "I'll be seeing you around." When he said those casual words, he didn't suspect that he would be seeing a lot of Willie Mays very soon.

Willie would have been quite content to spend the 1951 season at Minneapolis, especially after the rousing start he made there. After the first 35 games, he was hitting an amazing .477 — almost one hit for every two times at bat. He had already scored 38 runs, better than one per game, and hit eight home runs. The Minneapolis fans adored him, and some of the older writers in that city compared Willie favorably with another great hitter who had once played for Minneapolis — a fellow by the name of Ted Williams.

There was one unforgettable day in Milwaukee when Willie hit a line drive so hard that it struck the wooden outfield fence and went right through it. As the crowd gasped in disbelief, the umpire halted the game to try to figure out how many bases Willie was entitled to. The hole in the fence became such a curiosity that, instead of repairing it, the Milwaukee management painted a circle around it. And there it remained until the ball park was torn down several years later.

Willie was happy in Minneapolis. People called him by his name on the street and he was welcome everywhere. He had even started to date a Minneapolis girl. But his days in that city were numbered.

One afternoon toward the end of May, when the team had a day off, Willie went to see a movie. In fact, he went to a double feature. But he saw only one film because the house lights went on before the second movie began.

"If Willie Mays is here," said a man from the stage, "his manager wants him at the hotel immediately."

Willie was puzzled by this urgent summons, but he hurried from the theater to the nearby hotel and knocked on the door of the manager's room. It was a smiling Tommy Heath who opened the door and thrust out his hand. "Congratulations, Willie!" he shouted. "You're going to the big leagues."

Willie stared at him, then blurted out, "Who said so?"

Heath looked puzzled. "Why Leo told me himself," he said. "I talked to him on the phone not a half-hour ago."

"Well, you just call him right back and tell him I'm not coming," Willie said.

The manager could hardly believe his ears.

Willie Mays keeps his eye on the ball. As center fielder for the Giants' Minneapolis farm team, he batted .477.

Every minor leaguer dreamed of getting the call to the big leagues, and here was a .477 hitter saying he didn't want to go! He tried to reason with Willie. He even argued with him, but Willie was firm.

"I'm happy here," he said, "and I don't think I can hit big-league pitching anyhow."

Heath gulped and answered, "O.K., Willie, but I'm not going to be the one to tell Durocher you won't go. You're going to have to tell him yourself."

A few minutes later, Willie held the phone away from his ear as a furious Leo Durocher gave him a piece of his mind. Finally, when Durocher had calmed down a little, he barked, "What do you mean, you're not coming up?"

"I mean, I can't play that kind of ball. I can't hit big-league pitching," Willie answered.

There was a pause. "What are you hitting right now?" Durocher asked.

"Four seventy-seven," said Willie.

There was a longer pause. "Do you think," said Durocher quietly, "that you can hit .250 for me?"

"Two fifty?" Willie repeated. "I think so."

"Well," said Durocher, his voice starting

to rise again, "then get up here — right away!"

Willie stopped at his room just long enough to shove his baseball shoes and glove into a little canvas bag, grab his favorite bat, and jam a plaid golfer's cap on his head. Manager Heath had promised to pack the rest of Willie's clothes and send them along later.

Willie had time for only one quick telephone call before hurrying out to the taxi that would take him to the airport. He called the girl he had been dating and explained his sudden departure.

"I guess that means I'll never see you again," she said sadly.

"Don't be so sure," Willie answered. "I'll probably be back here by next week."

He was wrong, though. For Willie Mays, just turned twenty years old, would never wear a minor-league uniform again.

5

Rookie Center Fielder of the Giants

WILLIE was still wearing his colorful golfer's cap and carrying a bat when he walked into the offices of the New York Giants on busy 42nd Street in Manhattan. A secretary rushed him into Horace Stoneham's office and the Giants' president rose and shook his hand. "Welcome to New York, Willie," he said. "I'm glad you could make it so soon. Do you have any luggage?"

"No, sir," Willie replied. "It's still back in Minneapolis."

"Don't worry about it," Stoneham said. "I'll give you some money and you can buy enough clothes to hold you in Philadelphia."

"In Philadelphia?" Willie asked.

"That's where the team is, and that's where you're going," Stoneham answered. He pressed a button on his desk and said into the intercom, "Send Doc in here."

In a few moments the door opened and a wiry, red-faced man appeared. Stoneham introduced Willie to Doc Bowman, the Giants' trainer who would escort him to Philadelphia. Willie was impressed by the treatment he was getting from the president of the New York Giants.

"Thank you, Mr. Stoneham," he said as he headed for the door. "I hope I can get into a few games and help out."

Stoneham stared at him in surprise. "Help out?" he repeated. "Willie, don't you know you're starting in center field tonight?"

Now it was Willie's turn to stare in surprise. He was going to be the starting center fielder of the New York Giants! And he didn't even have a uniform.

All the way from New York to Philadelphia, Willie stared out of the window of the Pullman car and wondered what it would be like. He was thrilled, yet he was scared, too. Were they expecting too much from him? What if he should fall on his face?

Luckily, the trip was a short one, and Willie perked up a bit as the train passed through Trenton. He realized that some of the fans who had watched him play there the year before would probably be in Philadelphia to watch him play that night. That made him feel a little better.

In Philadelphia, Doc Bowman took Willie to the hotel where the Giants were staying and Willie was delighted to find that he would be sharing a room with Monte Irvin, an old friend from barnstorming days. But he barely had time to say hello to Irvin before he was whisked to the suite where Leo Durocher was waiting. The Giants' manager, who always traveled with a complete wardrobe of clothes, grinned at Willie's informal costume, topped by the zany golf cap.

"I haven't got any other clothes," Willie started to explain.

Durocher waved his hand for Willie to stop. "Never mind that," he snapped. "Did you bring a bat?"

"Yes," Willie replied.

"A glove?"

"Yes."

"Spikes?"

"Yes."

"Then you came to play," Durocher said happily, "and son, am I glad to see you."

The words made Willie feel good. He didn't know, though, how much Durocher was speaking from the heart. For the Giants' manager liked to play hunches, and now he was about to play one of the biggest hunches of his long baseball career. He was gambling on Willie, who had never played a minute of major-league baseball, to provide the spark the Giants needed to win the National League pennant.

So far, it had been a rough season for the Giants. Favored to make a powerful race, they had begun the season by losing 11 straight games. Since then, they had played quite well, winning 16 of their next 23 games. Now they were in fifth place, but Leo Durocher was still unhappy because the club had lost five of its first six games against his old team, the Brooklyn Dodgers. Could Willie give the Giants the boost that Durocher wanted?

For the first time, on the evening of May 25, 1951, in Philadelphia, Willie Mays stepped up to the plate, wearing a Giants' uniform with the numeral "24" on the back. The Phillies' pitcher was Emory "Bubba" Church and the result was an inglorious strikeout. It was the beginning of a bad evening for Willie. He failed to hit in five times at bat. Later, in the outfield, he crashed into his new roommate, Monte Irvin, while chasing a long drive by Eddie Waitkus that went for a double. But the Giants won the game, and the clubhouse was a noisy and cheerful place as Willie slipped out of his new uniform.

The next day Willie didn't get a hit, but the Giants won again. The same thing happened on the third day. Willie had now been up twelve times without a hit, but the Giants had yet to lose with him in the line-up. It didn't seem to make any sense to Willie, but nobody had mentioned his failure to hit. In fact, Leo Durocher seemed to go out of his way to joke with him and pat him on the back. Anyone would have thought that Willie was the team hero.

"I don't know why Mr. Durocher keeps me in there," Willie said to Monte Irvin as they got ready to return to New York with the team after the third game. "I haven't done a thing so far."

Irvin just laughed. "Look, roomie," he said. "We just swept a series from the team that won the pennant last year and we're playing .500 ball now. You may not be doing anything out there, but you're sure bringing us luck. And as long as we keep winning, Durocher isn't about to bench you."

Willie's name was in the starting line-up the next night at the Polo Grounds against the Boston Braves. He gulped hard when he saw the name of the Braves' pitcher. It was Warren Spahn, rated as the best left-handed pitcher in the league.

The New York fans gave Willie a solid round of applause when his name was announced before the game. But it was nothing compared to the thunder of clapping hands when he stepped into a Spahn pitch in the very first inning and drove it into the stands for a home run — his first hit as a Giant. Unfortunately, it was the only run the team could score off Spahn as the Braves won the game 4-1.

After the home run, Willie went to the plate thirteen more times without getting a hit. His Giants' batting average dove to .039. Still, Durocher made no move to replace Willie in center field. If he wasn't hitting, at least he was performing some great feats in the outfield. Durocher admired the way that Willie could take off at the crack of the bat, speed to where the ball would land, and then stand there, pounding his fist into his glove, until the ball came down.

Durocher was a smart manager and he realized that Willie Mays would start to hit eventually. All of the reports he had read on his new player stressed the fact that he hit in streaks. Durocher was willing to wait.

The only one discouraged by Willie's performance was Willie himself. After one game, he felt so bad that he sat down in front of his locker and cried. Coach Herman Franks saw him and went to tell Leo Durocher. In a moment the manager was at Willie's side. "Mr. Leo, send me back down," Willie blurted out. "I told you I couldn't hit this pitching."

"Listen to me," said Durocher. "So you haven't been hitting. So what? Everybody has slumps. Have we been winning ball games since you got here?"

"I guess so," Willie mumbled.

"You're darn right we have," growled the manager, "and you're my center fielder. That's that."

In later years Willie Mays would say that Leo Durocher gave him the one thing he needed to be a great player — confidence. And no player ever needed a dose of confidence more than Willie did that night in the Giants' clubhouse.

The next night was different. Willie got two hits — a single and a triple — as the Giants beat Pittsburgh. The next day he got two doubles against St. Louis and scored the only run in a 1-0 Giant victory. After getting only one hit in his first 26 times at bat,

Willie collected nine in his next 24, to move his average up to .200. By the end of June, he had put together a ten-game hitting streak and added six more home runs to his total.

By July, with Willie hitting steadily and the Giants winning regularly, the team had climbed into second place. But the Dodgers were so far ahead that most of the baseball writers and even some of the Giant fans were conceding the pennant to Brooklyn.

Only Leo Durocher wasn't having any part of it. He made one last adjustment to what he later called "my kind of team." Bobby Thomson, the good-looking Scotsman, had been moved from center field to left field to make room for Willie Mays. Now Durocher moved Bobby Thomson to third base to replace the weak-hitting Hank Thompson. Into left field went Monte Irvin. With Irvin and Don Mueller on either side of Mays, Durocher had the makings of an excellent outfield. And with two hard-hitting former outfielders — Thomson and Whitey Lockman — in the infield, the Giants boasted stronger hitting power.

These changes improved the team's performance but on August 11, the Dodgers still led the Giants by thirteen-and-a-half games, with less than a third of the season remaining. Then things began to happen.

Suddenly, the Giants forgot how to lose. They won sixteen straight games to cut the Dodgers' lead to five games. Willie Mays did his share of hitting in those victories. He also turned in a defensive play that still ranks as one of the best ever seen on a baseball field.

It came in a game against the Dodgers at the Polo Grounds. The score was tied at 1-1 in the eighth inning when the Dodgers made their victory bid. With Billy Cox, a fast man, on third base, hard-hitting Carl Furillo came to bat. Willie swung over a little toward left field, where the right-handed Furillo could be expected to hit. Instead, Furillo failed to hit the ball solidly and sent a fly ball toward the wide gap between Mays and right fielder Mueller.

Willie reacted immediately, turning and running for the ball. It was obvious that he would catch it after a hard run, but Cox was already tagging up at third base to score after the catch. It was an impossible situation for Willie, a right-handed thrower. For he was running in the wrong direction to get off a fast throw to home plate. If he stopped after the catch and turned around and threw, there wasn't a chance to keep Cox from scoring. Any other outfielder would have made the catch and conceded the run. But Willie Mays isn't just any other outfielder.

Running toward the wall, he stuck up his gloved left hand to catch the ball and in almost the same motion, shoveled it into his right hand and pivoted sharply on his left foot. This had the effect of spinning him completely around. As he came out of the spin facing the infield, his arm was cocked to throw. First baseman Lockman moved into position between Mays and the plate to act as the cut-off man, and Willie fired.

The ball came directly at Lockman like a small white cannonball and the first baseman made a quick decision. He stepped aside and let the ball go through to home plate, where catcher Wes Westrum waited. The ball came in perfectly and Westrum tagged the sliding Cox for the third out as the crowd roared.

On the Dodger bench, manager Charley Dressen blinked and shook his head. After the game he told reporters, "I saw it and I still don't believe it. He'll have to do it again before I'll believe it."

Even though the Giants were the hottest team in baseball in the final weeks of the

1951 season, the league-leading Dodgers refused to crack. By mid-September, when the Giants traveled to Brooklyn for their last two scheduled meetings with the Dodgers, they were still trailing by five-and-a-half games. In the first game, Dodgers' pitching ace Don Newcombe beat the Giants with a two-hit shutout, building the Dodgers' lead to six-and-a-half games. It didn't look as though the Giants could ever overcome the Brooklyn lead.

Dodger fans didn't think so. Ebbets Field was filled for the first game, but the stands were half-empty for the second. The Giants' Sal Maglie won his twentieth game of the season by eking out a 2-1 victory, but nobody cared — except the Giants.

With little more than a week remaining of the season, they grimly chipped away at the Dodgers' lead, reducing it to two-and-a-half games by September 25th. On that day the Giants defeated the Phillies for their thirty-fourth victory in forty-one games. When the Dodgers lost both games of a double-header in Boston, the lead was down to one game!

That one-game lead disappeared the next day as the Giants won again and the Dodgers lost. New York went absolutely baseball crazy and it was little wonder. The New York Yankees had already clinched the American League pennant. Now New York's two National League teams were tied for first place!

Willie Mays had never seen such excitement in his life — and the race for the National League pennant wasn't over yet.

On the next-to-last day of the season, the Giants shut out the Braves and Willie thrilled the crowd by stealing second and third base in the same inning. At the same time the Dodgers won in Philadelphia so the tie remained.

Then it was the last day of the season. Again the Giants beat the Braves 3-2. Willie and the rest of the Giants could hardly conceal their joy, especially when they learned that the Phillies were beating the Dodgers. But by the time the team reached the train that would take them back to New York, the situation had changed. The Dodgers had had a big rally to tie the game 8-8 and send it into extra innings. Sometime during the trip home, the final result was passed from player to player: the Dodgers' Jackie Robinson had hit a home run in the fourteenth inning to win the clutch game for Brooklyn.

The pennant race had ended in a tie. That

Catcher Roy Campanella tags Willie Mays out in one of the decisive games between the Giants and the Dodgers

meant there would have to be a play-off between the Giants and the Dodgers to decide the National League championship.

The rules called for a best two-out-of-three-game play-off series. In the first game Jim Hearn pitched the Giants to a 3-1 victory. But the next day, at the Polo Grounds, the Dodgers threw rookie pitcher Clem Labine at the Giants and won easily 10-0. That meant the third game would decide the champion. Both teams had their best pitchers ready: Sal Maglie for the Giants and Don Newcombe for the Dodgers.

There wasn't an empty seat in the Polo Grounds on the afternoon of October 3rd as the Giants and Dodgers squared off for the last game.

The Dodgers scored a run in the first inning and made it hold up for six innings. In the seventh inning, the Giants managed to tie the game until the Dodgers jumped on Maglie for three runs in the eighth inning to take a 4-1 lead. The Giants failed to score in their half of the eighth inning.

It was still 4-1 as the Giants got ready for the last half of the ninth inning. Before he left the dugout to take his usual place in the third-base coaching box, Durocher turned to his players and said, "All right, we've come this far and we've still got a chance."

Alvin Dark was the first batter for the Giants. He hit a hard ground ball that got between first baseman Gil Hodges and second baseman Jackie Robinson for a single. Don Mueller was the next batter and he hit a ball in almost the same place with the same result, as Dark stopped at second base. Now it was Monte Irvin's turn, but the best he could do was a foul fly that was caught without the runners being able to move up a base. Now there was one out with runners on first and second, and the Dodger infield swung around to try for the double-play that would end the game and the season.

But the Giants were not ready to be counted out yet. Whitey Lockman hit a double to left field that let Dark score from second base and sent Mueller to third. The score was 4-2 as Bobby Thomson walked to the plate and Willie Mays took his place in the on-deck circle. He could feel his heart pounding with excitement as he waited for his turn at bat.

It was then that Willie saw Dodger manager Dressen walk slowly out to the pitcher's mound and gesture to the bullpen. He was removing the tiring Newcombe from the game and bringing in Ralph Branca, a well-rested and strong-armed relief pitcher. Willie watched Branca warming up, and suddenly a thought crossed his mind: What if the Dodgers decided to walk Thomson intentionally to fill the bases, and then pitch to him instead? The thought made Willie's heart beat faster than ever.

But the first pitch to Thomson was a fast ball right down the middle and the umpire yelled, "Stee-rike!" Branca had no intention of walking Thomson, and he threw the next pitch in the same spot. This time Thomson wasn't keeping his bat on his shoulder. He took a big swing, connected solidly, and the ball rose high into the sky before settling into the left-field stands for a three-run homer to win the game for the Giants 5–4.

Willie leaped into the air as the Polo Grounds burst into sound. He couldn't have been happier if he had hit the home run himself. The Giants had done the impossible. They had won the game and the pennant, and this was what Willie wanted most.

6

Bring on the Yankees

THE Giants didn't have much time to celebrate their miracle finish. The very next afternoon they crossed the Harlem River and entered nearby Yankee Stadium to begin the World Series. Some people thought it was unfair that the Giants, who had just finished three tough play-off games, had to play the well-rested Yankees without even a single day off. But the Giants' players didn't complain. They preferred starting the World Series while the team was still cheered by its victory over Brooklyn.

There were 70,000 people in Yankee Stadium for the opening game. Red, white, and blue bunting decorated the railings, giving the place a gay holiday look. The other players in the dugout pointed out to Willie famous actors, politicians, and personal friends in the crowd. But Willie's eyes were on the field where the Yankees were having their pregame warm-up. He quickly located the tall man with number five on his back — his idol, Joe DiMaggio! Willie was seeing him in the flesh for the first time.

Willie wanted to go over and just say hello to DiMaggio. But he held back. He was too shy to approach him before so many people — the man he had so admired and copied when he was a boy. Besides, newspapermen and photographers were swarming around the Yankee star. Willie had just decided to stay where he was, when one of the photographers came running over.

"Hey, Willie, come on over and pose with DiMag," he said.

Willie gave his high-pitched laugh and replied, "Aw, why would he want to be in the same picture with me?"

But he went along anyway and had a chance to chat for a minute with his hero, as the flashbulbs popped all around them. Neither Willie nor the photographers realized that this was a historic moment. For DiMaggio, tired and aching at the age of thirty-six, had already secretly decided to retire after the World Series. In shaking hands with Willie Mays, one of the greatest

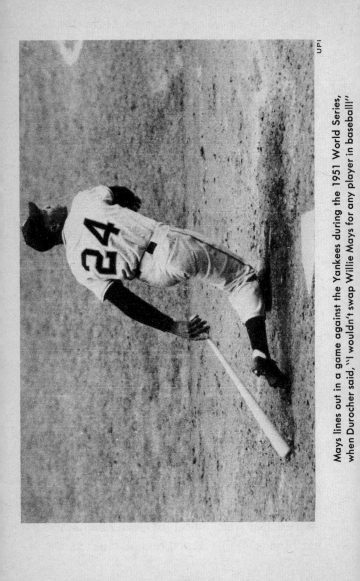

Mays lines out in a game against the Yankees during the 1951 World Series, when Durocher said, "I wouldn't swap Willie Mays for any player in baseball!"

stars of his era was greeting one of the greatest stars of the future.

Another great future star on the field that day was Mickey Mantle. Earlier in the season the Yankees had begun grooming this exciting young outfielder to take DiMaggio's place in center field. For years to come Mays and Mantle would be the names most often mentioned whenever the question arose: who was the best center fielder in baseball? But during this World Series, it was still DiMaggio.

The Giants started off the World Series in the same high spirits they had shown against Brooklyn. They beat the Yankees in the first game 5-1 as Willie's roommate, Monte Irvin, got four hits and Alvin Dark hit a three-run homer. But the Yankees came back to win the second game 3-1 and tie the Series; Willie didn't get a hit.

The Giants came roaring back to win the third game 6-2 as Willie made his best contribution of the Series: two hits and a run batted in. The fourth game was scheduled for the Polo Grounds, and the Yankees announced their pitcher would be Johnny Sain. The Giants thought they had a chance to win against Sain's pitching. The Giants had hit him freely several times earlier in the season when he was pitching for the Boston Braves. They were confident they could do it again. But they never got the chance.

The fourth game was scheduled for Sunday afternoon, and it poured that day, causing a postponement. When the teams met the next day it was not Sain but the Yankees' ace, Allie Reynolds, who walked out to the pitcher's mound. With the aid of a two-run homer by DiMaggio, the Yankees won 6-2 and again the Series was tied.

The fifth game wasn't even close, as the Yankees clouted the Giants 13-1. The Giants, however, made a gallant effort to pull out the sixth game. Trailing 4-1, they rallied in the ninth inning to score two runs, and they might have scored again except for a brilliant diving catch by Yankee outfielder Hank Bauer, who made the third out on his knees. The wild, unbelievable 1951 season had ended at last.

As Willie packed his bags to return to Alabama, he felt a little disappointed with his performance. In 121 games with the Giants, he had batted .274, with 20 home runs and 68 runs batted in. It wasn't a bad record for a rookie, but Willie worried about the slump that had overtaken him late in the season — a slump which had hung on through the play-offs with Brooklyn and the World Series. In the six World Series games, he had been able to get only four singles in 22 times at bat, a .182 average.

He would have felt better if he could have heard Leo Durocher's angry reply to a baseball writer who questioned Willie's performance. "Don't tell me his batting average!" Durocher roared. "Tell me how many games he won for us in a year when just one more loss would have cost us the pennant. All I know is, we were in fifth place when Willie joined us, and we were in first when the season ended. I wouldn't swap Willie Mays for any player in baseball!"

Most of the baseball writers agreed with Durocher, and voted Willie the National League's Rookie of the Year.

Willie's return to Fairfield, Alabama, was a joyful homecoming. There were parties and get-togethers with his old friends and relatives, and Willie splurged with his World Series check. Most of it went to buy his father a car, but there was enough left for Willie to buy some clothes and a portable phonograph that he had wanted for a long time.

Willie was beginning to enjoy the life of a celebrity when the notice from his draft board arrived.

7

Private Willie Mays

WILLIE MAYS wasn't very happy when he
reported to the Giants' spring training camp
at Phoenix, Arizona, early in 1952. He was
due to be drafted into the Army very soon,
and perhaps sent to Korea. Willie felt it was
his patriotic duty to go. After all, he was
twenty years old and single, just as most of
the other draftees were. But he was worried
about his Aunt Sarah and his other relatives
whom he had been helping to support, ever
since he had begun to make money playing
baseball.

Willie's mother had remarried after di-
vorcing his father, and she now had ten children with her second husband. The children
idolized Willie, and he tried to help them by
sending money to provide for their upbring-
ing and education whenever he could. His
stepfather didn't make much money. And

neither did Aunt Sarah, who often needed money to pay medical bills.

Willie told the draft board in Birmingham about the number of relatives who depended on him for support. They listened but ruled that none of the people that Willie was helping was closely enough related to him to keep him from going into the Army. Willie didn't like the ruling. He felt it was unfair, but there was nothing he could do about it.

Willie was due to be inducted into the Army in May, only a month after the 1952 season opened. Some of his friends thought that Willie shouldn't bother going through the tough training-camp period just to play a few weeks of baseball. But Willie wouldn't listen. He arrived at Phoenix with the rest of his teammates and announced that he would play as long as he could.

Although many baseball experts had picked the Giants to win the National League pennant in 1952, others had doubts. Eddie Stanky, the fiery second baseman of the "miracle" team, was no longer with the Giants. He had signed a contract to manage the St. Louis Cardinals. And Mays would be leaving soon. Could the Giants afford to lose two such valuable men in the same season?

Leo Durocher wasn't happy about these

losses but he thought the Giants could get by without Stanky and Mays. He pointed out that young Davey Williams, who had been groomed to succeed Stanky, was an excellent second baseman. And Bobby Thomson, who had played center field before Willie Mays joined the team, could always go back to his old position.

Then, just before the season started, the Giants' pennant hopes for 1952 suffered another bad jolt. In an exhibition game against the Cleveland Indians at Denver, Colorado, Willie came up to hit with Monte Irvin on first base. Willie promptly hit a single and ran to first base. At most times, Irvin would have stopped at second base because Willie usually hit the ball to left field, and it would be an easy matter for the left fielder to throw Irvin out at third base. But this time Willie had hit the ball to right field and Irvin decided that he had a good chance to beat the long throw from the right fielder. So he rounded second base and roared into third with a slide.

From the other side of the diamond, Willie heard the sickening crack of a breaking bone and saw Irvin rolling in pain on the ground. The umpire immediately raised his hands in the signal for time, while Willie raced across the diamond to his roommate's side. Just a glance at Irvin's foot, dangling from his leg at an odd angle, told Willie that Irvin had broken his ankle. He wouldn't be able to play for months, possibly not for the entire season.

Willie couldn't help himself. As he kneeled beside his injured friend, he burst out crying, for in the year that they had roomed together, Irvin had become his closest friend. Monte, who was twelve years older than Willie, had taken the place of the big brother that Willie never had. He had given Willie advice on cars, clothes, places to eat, even on dating.

When the team was on the road, Monte had roomed and eaten with Willie. He would go to the movies with him, or grumble good-naturedly about the records Willie liked to play on his portable phonograph.

When the team was home in New York, Willie had been a frequent guest at the Irvins' home in New Jersey. Sometimes Monte would spend an evening in New York with Willie, and the children in the Harlem neighborhood where Willie lived would be treated to a rare sight — two major-league ballplayers playing stickball.

It had been Monte Irvin, as much as Leo

Willie Mays with teammate Monte Irvin. Irvin roomed with
Willie when the team traveled and was like a big brother.

Durocher, who had given Willie confidence during his first weeks with the Giants, when everything seemed to be going wrong.

Now, as Willie watched his roommate being gently placed on a stretcher and carried from the field, he thought of all the good times they had shared. For Willie, the days ahead were going to be even tougher without Monte.

The days ahead were also going to be hard for the rest of the Giants. Leo Durocher, when asked what effect the loss of Irvin would have on the team, answered, "I don't know. We might be able to get along without Mays or without Irvin. But without both of them? I just don't know."

Willie was able to play in thirty-four games for the Giants before reporting for Army service. Although he hit only .236 and four home runs, the Giants won twenty-seven of the thirty-four games and were in first place on May 28. That was the day Willie played his last game against the Dodgers at Brooklyn. He didn't get a hit, but he did get a remarkable tribute from the Dodger fans — who usually saved their loudest boos for the Giants. As Willie stepped up to the plate for the last time, the Dodger fans rose and applauded him loudly. Willie stood at the plate, fidgeting nervously as the clapping continued and wondering what he should do. Then he glanced over at the Giants' dugout. All of his teammates were also on their feet, clapping. And so were the Dodgers in their dugout. It was a moment that Willie would cherish for a long time.

It was a moment that the Giants would look back at wistfully. Three days later they had dropped behind the Dodgers into second place. Then they proceeded to lose six of their next eight games before Durocher managed to get them winning again. But by then it was too late. Without Mays and Irvin for most of the season, the Giants finished in second place, four-and-a-half games behind the Dodgers.

Willie followed the rest of the 1952 season from Fort Eustis, Virginia, where he was assigned by the Army. At the camp, Willie was made a physical education instructor. It was a fairly simple assignment, and Willie found plenty of time to play for the camp baseball team. There were two other young major leaguers on the team, pitcher Vernon Law of the Pittsburgh Pirates and outfielder Karl Olson of the Boston Red Sox. The team played frequent games with other service teams in the area, as well as with good semipro teams.

In his spare time, Willie experimented with his fielding. He practiced holding his glove the way a first baseman does, with only the fingers inside. This made the glove into a sort of claw that extended several inches beyond the end of his fingers. Willie found that when he had mastered the trick of catching a baseball in the claw he could reach balls that once would have gone over his head. He has used this technique ever since that time.

Another thing that Willie practiced was the waist-high or *basket* catch. Willie had caught balls like that back in Fairfield as a boy. Later he learned how to catch fly balls in the regular way, with the glove at eye level so that he could watch the ball at all times. It was the sight of a young soldier catching the ball at his waist during a physical training session that interested Willie again in the basket catch.

As the instructor, Willie had tried to point out to the soldier that his method was wrong. The youngster, who had never caught a ball any other way, looked doubtful. So Willie borrowed a glove and asked the soldier to throw several balls high in the air while he caught each one at eye level.

Private Willie Mays of the U. S. Army. After basic training, Willie was physical education instructor at Fort Eustis, Virginia, and played ball for the camp team.

"All right," the soldier said. "But now try it my way."

So Willie caught a few balls at his waist and was actually surprised to discover that he felt more comfortable with the waist-high style. He found that he could position his feet for a throw even before he had caught the ball. Willie tried the basket catch in some service games and liked it so well that he decided to catch that way in the future.

During one service game, Willie stole a base with Fort Eustis leading by 14-0. It is a baseball tradition that a player doesn't steal a base when his team has a big lead because of the chance of injury. When Leo Durocher got word of what Willie had done he was furious. He managed to get a phone call through to Willie at the camp. About the only line that Willie heard clearly above all the sputtering and fuming was: "Are you out of your mind?"

There was another angry call from Durocher that winter, when Willie decided to play a little basketball for the Fort Eustis team. After he sprained an ankle, Durocher informed Willie that his basketball days were over. Willie Mays, the Giants' manager said, was to be strictly a baseball player and nothing else.

The 1953 season was a disaster for the Giants without Mays. For the first few months the team hung on gamely, but by July they began to slip. By August, when a reporter asked manager Charley Dressen of the league-leading Dodgers whether he thought the Giants were a threat, he answered, "The Giants is dead!" The team finally ended up in fifth place, losing forty-four of their last sixty-four games.

Leo Durocher offered no alibis for the Giants. But he pointed out to sportswriters that Willie would be out of the Army in time to play the entire 1954 season.

"Willie will make us well again," he promised.

The long countdown of days of Army service finally ended in March 1954. Almost two years after he had been inducted, Willie Mays walked out the front gate of Fort Eustis, with his discharge papers in his pocket. He was met by Frank Forbes, a Giants' scout and an old friend from New York. Forbes drove Willie to the Washington airport and put him on a plane to Phoenix, where the Giants were in training.

8

Return to Glory

WILLIE MAYS could hardly wait to see the familiar faces of his old teammates, and hear their friendly jokes and wisecracks. What he didn't know was that the Giants had decided to have some fun with their returning star.

Most of the players were already out on the playing field when Willie walked into the clubhouse and approached the attendant, who had been with the Giants for years.

"Say hey!" shouted Willie. "I'm here!"

The attendant looked at him blankly and said, "What's your name?"

"It's me!" shrieked Willie. "Don't you remember me?"

The attendant examined the team roster. Finally he looked and said, "You're Mays, aren't you? We'll give you a uniform. Number twenty-four. Get dressed quickly and get out there. The extra men hit first."

"What do you mean, 'the extra men'?" demanded the thoroughly confused Willie.

"You weren't here last year, so you're an extra man," the attendant answered. "You'd better hurry-up. You're late already."

Willie undressed quickly and was beginning to pull on his uniform when pitcher Sal Maglie came into the clubhouse, perspiring from a workout. He walked right past Willie, gave him a brief glance, then asked the attendant, "Who's that? Some new rookie?"

It was the same thing when Willie got out on the field. Leo Durocher was standing beside the batting cage, watching the hitters, and he only grunted when Willie came running up with a high-pitched greeting.

"Okay, twenty-four," growled Durocher. "Let's see you hit."

Willie grabbed a bat and practically leaped into the batting cage. The first pitch was right over the plate, and Willie took a full swing, driving it clear out of the park.

"Say, how about that," he said proudly.

No one said a word.

The next pitch was a good curve ball, and Willie hit that one out of the park, too. He wasn't sure what kind of a gag his teammates were playing on him, but he knew it felt awfully good to be hitting a baseball in a Giants' uniform again.

It wasn't until he had finished his turn in the batting cage that he noticed a cluster of people watching him — players, reporters, and photographers. Now they were all grinning broadly, waiting to give Willie a warm welcome back.

Afterward, Willie made his way to the dugout to see his old friend Monte Irvin. But no sooner had they started to talk, than Durocher came swooping in and picked Willie up in a bear hug.

"Welcome home, Willie!" he yelled. "It's going to be just like old times again!"

As it turned out, it was even better than old times. On opening day of the season, the Giants faced the Dodgers at the Polo Grounds and Willie hit a home run off Carl Erskine. Five days later, at Ebbets Field, he hit a second home run against Erskine. After that the home runs came fast for Willie.

By the end of May, Willie had fourteen home runs and the Giants were running neck-and-neck with the Dodgers for the league lead. The presence of Willie Mays in the line-up seemed to give the Giants a zip that had been missing since 1951, and a new spirit of confidence filled the team.

The Giants were playing exciting baseball, and one of their most spectacular plays
became the pinch home run. In Dusty
Rhodes, an outfielder who had joined the
team while Willie was in the Army, the
Giants boasted one of the most dangerous
pinch-hitters in the game. Time and again
that season, Rhodes would come up to the
plate in a tight spot and smash a baseball
out of the park.

In addition, the Giants were getting good
pitching from Sal Maglie, Johnny Antonelli
(who had been obtained from the Braves in
a trade for Bobby Thomson), and Ruben
Gomez. And when these pitchers got into
trouble, veterans like Hoyt Wilhelm and
Marvin Grissom were ready to come in from
the bullpen to stifle any enemy rallies.

But it was Willie Mays that the crowds
came to see and cheer. And Willie didn't dis-
appoint them. By the end of June, when the
Giants moved past the Dodgers into first
place, Willie was hitting .313 and had twenty-four home runs to his credit. By the end
of July, his home-run total had risen to
thirty-six. Some writers even began to
wonder if Willie might break Babe Ruth's
record of sixty home runs in a season.

Willie had become big news. Now the

whole country wanted to hear about baseball's newest superstar. Willie could hardly take a shower without some reporter or photographer trying to get an interview. He didn't dare go out on the street any more for a stickball game. A reporter was almost sure to pop up. There were constant invitations to appear on television shows, and Willie even had a song called "Say Hey, Willie" written about him.

The Giants, meanwhile, had become locked into a tight pennant race not only with their rivals, the Dodgers, but with the Milwaukee Braves, who suddenly came alive in mid-season. The Giants' lead, which had reached six-and-a-half games just before the All-Star Game in July, slowly began to crumble.

The trouble began a few days after the All-Star Game, when the Giants went into St. Louis for a series. Willie had just hit his thirty-second home run of the season off Cardinals' pitcher Vic Raschi, when bad news reached him from back home.

For weeks, he had known that his Aunt Sarah was dying of an incurable illness, and Willie had left word that he was to be called immediately if she became worse. Now, the brief message that she had died was relayed to him in the Giants' dugout. Tears filled Willie's eyes. His Aunt Sarah had actually been a mother to him, and even though he had tried to prepare himself for this news, he was overcome with grief when it came. As he sat with his head in his hands, Leo Durocher quietly motioned for a substitute to take Willie's place. That night, Willie was on a plane bound for Alabama and home.

Back in Fairfield, Aunt Sarah's house was surrounded by a crowd of curious spectators, anxious to see Willie and get his autograph. Willie shut himself into his old room to be alone with his grief.

Immediately after the funeral, Willie flew North to rejoin the team in Milwaukee. But some of the spark had gone out of him, and suddenly the Giants stopped winning. They lost three in a row to the Braves, then returned to New York and took a 9-1 beating from the Dodgers. The Giants' lead was down to three games.

On July 27th, the Giants lost to St. Louis 7-4, and the only consolation was Willie's thirty-fifth home run of the season — one of the longest of his career. It came in the ninth inning, with no one on base, and Cardinals' southpaw Harvey Haddix on the mound. Haddix decided that Willie was looking for a fast ball, so he gave him the fast-ball motion, then threw a slow change-up pitch. But Willie adjusted quickly and hit the pitch cleanly. The ball didn't stop traveling until it had nestled into the stands beyond the left-field bullpen at the Polo Grounds. The base of the wall at that point was 440 feet from home plate, and the ball went even farther, landing far up in the stands.

There was no celebration of the home run afterward. The Giants' defeat had reduced their lead to two games over the Dodgers. In the gloomy clubhouse Leo Durocher told the writers that the team had to start scoring more runs if it expected to hold on to first place. "I may have to make some changes in the line-up," he said grimly.

The next day Willie hit his thirty-sixth home run off Tom Poholsky as the Giants beat the Cardinals. But in the third game of the series, St. Louis shut out the Giants to win 8-0. Durocher was fit to be tied. The clubhouse door was locked as he angrily lectured the players after the game. Some of the players, tense and upset, shouted back at the manager.

The following day, Durocher called Willie into his office. The manager came directly to the point. "Willie, I want you to stop hitting homers."

Willie could hardly believe his ears. Stop hitting homers! Here he was, up among the leaders in home runs, and his own manager was telling him to stop.

"I know it sounds crazy," Durocher continued. "But I mean it. This team gets plenty of home runs, but it doesn't get consistent hitting. And that's where you come in. You're hitting .316 now. But if you swing for base hits, instead of homers, you can add thirty points to that before the season ends."

Durocher paused and then continued, "I'm moving you up to the third spot in the batting order today. All I want you to do is get on base as often as you can. We've got strong hitters coming up behind you who can bring you home. I'm not asking you to do this for me. I'm asking you to do it for the team. We're in a tough race and we need every run we can get."

Willie knew Durocher's words made sense. He thought for a few moments. Then the big smile appeared and he said, "O.K., Skip. I'll try it."

That night Willie stood in the batter's box and watched a good curve ball head for the plate. He could have given it a big home-run swing. Instead, he waited until the ball was almost past the plate and then swung his bat smoothly with just enough power to hit it cleanly into right field for a single. A few moments later, he had stolen second base. And a few moments after that, a teammate's hit sent Willie around third and sliding into home, as the crowd cheered. In the dugout, Willie looked over at Durocher, who was coaching at third base. The manager gave him a quick wink.

The Giants won that night, and then won five games in a row as Willie kept hitting singles and doubles to all fields. There weren't many home runs any more — Willie was to hit only six from that day to the end of the season — but the fans actually seemed to like the change. For now they could watch Willie run the bases, and that was a treat in itself as Willie teased the pitchers with long leads and head-first slides.

Not long after that, on August 8, 1954, came Willie Mays Day at the Polo Grounds.

Willie didn't really want the fans to make such a big fuss over him. He was embarrassed as he stood in the infield and heard one speaker after another praise him. Then came the gifts. Pretty soon a big table was loaded with them: an air conditioner, lug-

UPI

With his long arm reaching out, Willie Mays snatches a base hit away from the Dodger's Carl Furillo. Mays always made sensational catches look easy.

gage, a television set, jewelry. Willie could only mumble, "Thank you, thank you very much," as each gift was announced. And when he learned that the Polo Grounds ushers had chipped in to buy him a portable radio, and that his teammates had given him a tape recorder, Willie was so overwhelmed that he couldn't say anything. Finally, when the ceremonies were over, Willie tried to show the crowd how he felt by waving his cap and grinning. Then, as the Giants' fans stood and applauded, he fled into the dugout.

In the days ahead, Willie found his own way to say thanks to the Giants' fans — by hitting and winning ball games for his team. For example, there was one day late in August when the Giants lost a three-game series to the hated Dodgers and found themselves with a lead of only a half-game. No one on the team was happy. The players were too discouraged. But the day after the series ended, Willie smashed four hits against Philadelphia to lead the Giants to victory. That was the start of a seven-game winning streak that built the Giants' lead up to three games, and moved them on their way to the pennant.

The clinching victory was especially sweet because it was won against the Dodgers in

Brooklyn, and Willie got three hits to help make it possible.

After the pennant victory, attention shifted to the exciting race for the batting title, described in Chapter One; Willie, teammate Don Mueller, and the Dodgers' Duke Snider battled right down to the last day of the long season before Willie clinched the batting title with a .345 average.

"Willie, you've done it all," said a reporter after the last game. "You've won the batting title, led your team to the pennant, and you're a sure thing for Most Valuable Player. What's left for you to do?"

Willie grinned. "That's easy," he said. "We've got a World Series to play, and I hear that Cleveland team is pretty good."

9

Star of the Series

WILLIE was right. A very tough World Series faced the Giants in 1954. The Cleveland Indians had set an American League record by winning 111 of their 154 games. All but the most loyal New York sportswriters picked them as the favorites to defeat the Giants in the World Series.

For the first game in the Polo Grounds, the Indians named their best pitcher, Bob Lemon, to start. But Leo Durocher decided to play a hunch and didn't name his best pitcher. Instead of Johnny Antonelli, who had won twenty-one games and lost seven that season, Durocher picked Sal Maglie, a thirty-seven-year-old veteran with a 14-6 record. Maglie had a reputation for winning tough ball games, and Leo was sure that he would get a good pitching performance, win or lose.

Playing another hunch, Durocher inserted Willie Mays, who had been batting third, into the fourth spot in the Giants' batting order, between Don Mueller and Hank Thompson.

The score was tied at 2-2 in the eighth inning, when the Indians made their bid to win the ball game. Maglie was tired, and relief pitchers were already warming up in the Giants' bullpen as Doby walked and Rosen singled. That brought up Vic Wertz, who had already hit safely in his previous three turns at bat. Immediately Durocher sprang to his feet, signaling for a new pitcher. In came Don Liddle to pitch to the left-handed Wertz. In center field, Willie moved over to the right, ready to protect the area where Wertz had tripled in the first inning. He watched Liddle deliver a pitch, and saw the blur of Wertz's bat as he swung. Willie heard a sharp crack, and he could see the little white dot rising high above the grandstand and heading straight toward center field — the deepest part of the Polo Grounds.

Willie took one quick look at the ball, spun around, and ran at full speed toward the bleachers in center field. It was a long run from the point where he had originally stood. Willie kept moving fast until he felt

Racing back to catch Vic Wertz's drive in the 1954 World Series, Willie pivots, and powers the ball back quickly.

the crunch of cinders under his feet. He had reached the warning track, just a few feet from the wall. Only now did he take a quick look over his left shoulder. There was the ball, heading almost directly at him! Willie barely had time to get his glove up, but he caught the ball over his left shoulder while still running at full speed.

Even as he made the catch, Willie was thinking about Larry Doby, the Indians' runner on second base. Doby would certainly be able to move up to third base before Willie could return the ball to the infield, and there was also a good chance that he might try to go all the way and score. It was up to Willie to see that he didn't.

Quickly, he pulled the ball out of his glove, pivoted on his left foot, and whirled around to face the infield. He threw as hard as he could in the direction of home plate — and then his legs went out from under him and he fell sprawling. The ball traveled straight toward the cut-off man, second baseman Davey Williams, who caught it, then cocked his arm to relay it to home plate. But he didn't have to throw. Doby was standing on third base, making no attempt to go any further, and Rosen had scampered back to first. Like everybody else in the Polo

Grounds, Doby was shaking his head in disbelief. Willie Mays had just made one of the finest catches and throws ever seen in a World Series.

The Indians didn't score in that inning, and the score was still 2-2 as the game went into the tenth inning. Once again Vic Wertz stepped up to the plate. And once more Willie moved to the right. But this time, Wertz got his bat on a pitch that was slightly outside the plate and drove a line drive the wrong way for a left-handed hitter — between center and left fields. Willie had no chance to catch it. His concern now was to prevent the ball from rolling so far that Wertz might be able to run completely around the bases for an inside-the-park home run.

Running at full speed, Willie had only one thought: to somehow get between the ball and the wall. From the corner of his eye, he watched the flight of the ball and tried to guess where it would strike the ground. If he was lucky, the ball would bounce high and he would have a chance to cut it off cleanly. Instead, the ball didn't bounce high, but skipped a few inches off the ground. Desperately Willie thrust out his glove and grabbed it back-handed. By the time he was able to straighten up and throw the ball back to the infield, Wertz was on second base. But he didn't score and it was still a tie game as the Giants batted in the bottom of the tenth.

Willie was the second man to bat in that inning, and, as he kneeled in the on-deck circle, his alert eye noticed something unusual. The Indians had put a new catcher into the game, and that man's single practice throw to second base reached there on one bounce. Willie turned and spoke to Leo Durocher, who was just heading to his familiar place in the third-base coaching box.

"Hey Skip, can I try a steal if I get on base?" he asked.

Durocher looked surprised for a moment. Then he muttered, "Yeah." He had also noticed the poor throw and he understood that Willie wanted to take advantage of the catcher's weakness.

Lemon got the first man out, but he continued to pitch very carefully to Willie and gave him a base on balls. Moments later Willie made his move. Waiting for the instant that Lemon released a pitch to the next batter, Willie headed for second base as fast as his legs could carry him. As he had guessed, the throw from the catcher bounced in and he was safe.

Willie's bold move forced the Indians to change their tactics. Thompson was now intentionally given a base on balls so that Lemon could pitch to the less dangerous Monte Irvin. But Irvin never came to the plate. Instead, Durocher sent up his best pinch-hitter, Dusty Rhodes. And Rhodes delivered. He hit a lazy fly ball down the right-field line that just managed to get into the lower grandstand for a home run.

Willie had tagged up at second base, ready to go to third if the ball was caught. When he saw the umpire circling his hand over his head to indicate a home run, he jumped into the air and clapped his hands. Then he waved happily to Thompson to follow him as he ran around third base and leaped on home plate with the winning run.

In the dressing room after the game, everybody talked about Willie's great catch and Rhodes' pinch home run.

When a reporter asked him if the catch was the greatest he had ever made, Willie felt embarrassed and answered, "I don't rate 'em, I just catch 'em."

For the second game of the World Series, Johnny Antonelli started for the Giants and was in trouble with the very first pitch he threw. The Indians' lead-off hitter, Al

Smith, hit it out of the park for a home run. Antonelli got the next two men out, but then he walked Rosen and Wertz and that brought up Wally Westlake, who singled cleanly over second base. The hit should have scored Rosen from second base, but it didn't — because of Willie Mays. He came charging in from center field, scooped the ball up in his glove, and fired it perfectly to the catcher standing on home plate. Rosen stayed on third base as Antonelli finally got the third out.

The Indians' 1-0 lead seemed a threat as the first four innings went by and the Giants failed to get a man to first base. Then, in the fifth inning, Willie led off and drew a base on balls. The next batter, Hank Thompson, singled; Willie raced to third base; and the crowd suddenly came to life with a roar. Irvin was due to bat next, but Durocher played a hunch again and sent up Dusty Rhodes to pinch hit. This time, Rhodes hit a little fly ball over second base that landed just in front of the center fielder as Willie raced home with the tying run. Before the inning was ended, the Giants held a 2-1 lead. When the game was over, the Giants had won 3-1 on just four hits.

The Indians weren't quite the same team

after their two narrow defeats in New York. It was almost as though they knew they were going to lose the World Series.

When the Series moved to Cleveland for the third game, the Indians learned that Willie Mays could hurt them with his bat as well as with his glove. In the very first inning, with Mueller on second base, Willie swung at one of Mike Garcia's fast balls and singled, driving in the first Giants' run. It was Willie's first hit of the Series. In the sixth inning, with Whitey Lockman on second base, Willie singled again to drive in another run. That gave the Giants a big 6-0 lead. It was all they needed as they coasted to a 6-2 victory. And Willie had his third hit of the game when he singled again in the ninth inning.

Then came the fourth game. More than 78,000 people jammed the Cleveland Municipal Stadium, hoping to see the Indians come back.

The Giants scored two runs in the second inning. In the third inning, with two men on base, Willie chopped a double to left field and the score was 3-0. In the fifth inning, again with two men on base, Willie came up and this time drew a base on balls from the tiring Bob Lemon, who then left the game. The

Indians' relief pitcher walked Hank Thompson to force in one run, and then gave up a single to Irvin that scored two more. That made the score 7-0.

The game — and the World Series — ended 7-4. The amazing Giants had upset the favored Indians, and they had done it in four straight games!

On the plane back to New York, the players relaxed, drank champagne, and joked about their new role as World Champions. And when they landed at LaGuardia, over 2,500 fans roared their greeting. The round of celebrations that followed lasted right into the winter. And Willie Mays was the player that everyone wanted to see. He had dozens of invitations to attend banquets and appear on television. Honors poured in. He was named Most Valuable Player in the National League, Major League Player of the Year, Male Athlete of the Year, and Professional Athlete of the Year.

And everywhere Willie was asked about the catch he had made in the first game off Vic Wertz. He tried to explain honestly. The catch was not as difficult as it appeared, and he had made better catches in his career. His listeners always thought Willie was just being modest.

10

Good-by, New York

AFTER the 1954 World Series, Leo Durocher said, "Everything we did seemed to go right." But in 1955 nothing seemed to go right. The team's pitching went sour, its hitting dropped off, and frowns replaced smiles in the Giants' clubhouse. It was up to Willie Mays to lead the team out of its slump.

One day early in the season, Durocher took Willie aside and said, "I'm going to need you to hit the long ball this year, Willie. We're in trouble, and we need all the help we can get."

Willie nodded and began swinging for home runs again. It felt a little strange at first, because he had gotten used to hitting the ball squarely for singles and doubles. To hit home runs, he had to swing differently, timing his swing so that he could deliver all his power.

The fact that the Giants finished as high as third in 1955 was due mostly to Willie's hard hitting. He hit 51 home runs to lead the National League, batted in 127 runs, and finished the season with an excellent batting average of .319.

In center field, Willie continued to make amazing catches look easy. As a baserunner, he surprised opposing pitchers by stealing twenty-four bases — three times as many as he had stolen in 1954. He was named to play center field for the National League in the All-Star Game that was held in Milwaukee, and he astounded the crowd with a tremendous leap against the fence to take a home run away from the great Ted Williams. As it turned out, the catch won the game for the National League All-Stars, who defeated the American League All-Stars 6-5.

But even Willie Mays, as great as he was, found himself under pressure. Because the team wasn't winning, Willie sometimes tried too hard. Some days he wanted to get a hit so much that he'd swing at bad pitches and strike out. Both Durocher and coach Herman Franks had to keep telling Willie to take it easy.

There was one day when Willie stood on first base, thinking hard about getting to second base where he would be in better position to score a run. When the batter hit a fly ball to left field, Willie tagged up, ready to run to second base after the outfielder caught the ball. Only when he heard the coach shouting "No! No!" at him did he look again and realize that the outfielder was in a perfect position to throw directly to second base. After the game, Durocher was furious at him.

"Willie, were you really going to run on that catch?" he demanded.

"Yes, Skip. I thought I could make it," Willie admitted.

"You couldn't have made it if you flew to second base! All you would have gotten for us was another out!"

Then the manager's voice softened a little as he said, "Willie, you've been pressing too hard and it's starting to affect your playing. So I'm going to have to do something I've never done before. I'm going to bench you."

Willie was crushed. Not once, since he had joined the Giants, had he been taken out of the starting line-up while he had been present and in good health.

"How long will it be, Skip?" he asked.

"I don't know yet," said Durocher and he walked away.

The benching lasted only one day, but it gave Willie time to relax a little and to think about what he was doing wrong. Back in the starting line-up, a restored Willie was again hitting home runs and making sensational catches.

Still, it was the Brooklyn Dodgers and not the New York Giants who won the 1955 National League pennant and that was a blow to Willie. Another blow was the loss of the only major-league manager he had ever known.

Everyone in the baseball world was as surprised as Willie when the announcement came that Leo Durocher's contract as the Giants' manager was not being renewed for 1956. Willie had heard that Durocher and the team's owner, Horace Stoneham, weren't getting along. But it never occurred to him that he might some day have to play for any manager but Durocher, the man who had brought him to New York and given him the confidence he needed to become a star.

The new manager, Bill Rigney, was a nervous, scrappy little man whom Willie remembered as an infielder on the 1951 Giants. For the last two seasons he had been the manager at Minneapolis, and his team had won the American Association champion-

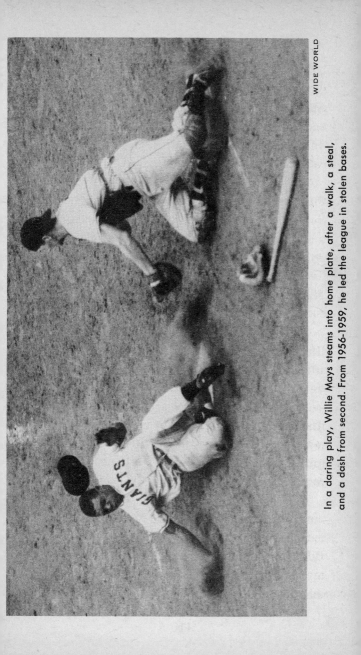

In a daring play, Willie Mays steams into home plate, after a walk, a steal, and a dash from second. From 1956-1959, he led the league in stolen bases.

ship in 1955. Willie and Rigney got along fine, but it wasn't the warm relationship that Willie and Durocher had had. Rigney recognized that Willie was an outstanding player, but he treated him like any other player on the team.

There was another big change in Willie's life in 1956. He married a beautiful woman named Marghuerite Wendell and bought a house in nearby Queens. There were no more stickball street games in Harlem. Now Willie bought a lawnmower and golf clubs, and did his best to settle down into married life.

The Giants started the 1956 season badly. In one of their early games with Brooklyn, Dodger pitcher Carl Erskine threw a no-hitter against them. Only two men managed to reach first base for the Giants. One of them was Willie Mays. For most of the early part of the season, the Giants were in last place while the Dodgers were among the league leaders.

Willie started hitting late in the season and the Giants surged into sixth place. But some of their fans were unhappy and blamed Willie for the team's poor showing.

Actually, Willie had done quite well. He had hit .296, and his total of thirty-six home runs was quite respectable. He had even led the league in stolen bases with forty.

The fault didn't lie with Willie, but with the rest of the team. As good players got old or were traded to other teams, their replacements simply were not as good. When the Giants made a trade during the winter of 1956 for veteran Dodger star, Jackie Robinson, some sportswriters predicted that Robinson would help the Giants win again.

But Robinson decided to retire and explained, quite honestly, "I don't see how I could help the Giants. That ball club needs rebuilding. It needs youth. It doesn't need me."

The Giants in 1957 were largely a veteran team, except for the twenty-six-year-old Willie Mays in center field. Once more he was the best of all the Giants. Now more relaxed under manager Rigney, he batted .333, with 35 home runs, 97 runs batted in, and 38 stolen bases.

Then, in May 1957, the National League approved the transfer of the New York Giants to San Francisco, California, and the Brooklyn Dodgers to Los Angeles. In 1958 it would be the San Francisco Giants and the Los Angeles Dodgers.

The Giants' last game at the old Polo

Grounds should have been a sad one, but it turned, instead, into a mad one. A crowd of about 11,000 fans turned out, partly to say good-by to the team, and partly to gather souvenirs from the old ball park, which was to be torn down.

The players in the Giant dugout watched the crowd nervously. People began swarming out of the grandstand in the last inning and headed toward the field. The people were not just autograph hunters. They were after souvenirs, too — anything they could carry away. Willie came to bat in the ninth inning, and as soon as it was over, he and his teammates ran wildly to the safety of the clubhouse, just ahead of the crowd.

From inside, Willie and the other players watched the mob. They ripped up seats, bases, home plate, and even pieces of turf, before a squad of policemen could shoo them out of the park. Many of the players lost caps, gloves, or jackets which they had left behind in their hasty flight from the field.

Later, Willie looked at the monogram of the letters "NY" on his blue Giants' cap, and summed up the bitter, sad feelings of the team when he said, "I guess all these are good for now is just souvenirs. Good-by, New York."

11

Hello, San Francisco

LEAVING New York City had been bad
enough. But now, here was Willie Mays playing for the very first time in San Francisco,
and the fans were booing him! Not all, of
course, but enough for Willie to hear them
as he trotted out to center field. The Giants
were playing in little Seals Stadium, a
minor-league park that they were using until their big new stadium was finished. It
was opening day of the 1958 season and the
San Francisco Giants, formerly of New
York, were playing the Los Angeles Dodgers, formerly of Brooklyn. Every seat in
Seals Stadium was filled.

Willie had first noticed the boos when the
team was introduced before the game. He
had just grinned good-naturedly. He figured
that some of the fans were just teasing him.
But as the game wore on, his smile turned to

a frown. Why were they still booing him? Willie looked around. It was a perfect spring afternoon, the Giants were shutting out the Dodgers, and Willie had already batted in two runs with a pair of singles. Then Willie heard a loud voice yelling at him from the stands: "What's the matter, Mays! Can't you hit a home run in this park? Did you leave all your homers in New York?"

But it wasn't just homers they wanted. They'd booed him from the beginning. Willie was puzzled, and he was bothered.

When the game was over he determined to find out why the San Francisco fans didn't like him. A local sportswriter came over to talk to him, and Willie got to the point immediately.

"I had a pretty good game," he said. "I don't expect cheers, but I sure don't expect boos, either. What's going on?"

The sportswriter looked embarrassed. "It doesn't have anything to do with the way you play, Willie," he said. "It's just that your name is Willie Mays, and the fans here think of you as a big star from New York. They resent all the build-up you've gotten, and as far as they're concerned you're an outsider playing in the very spot where their greatest hero played."

For a moment, Willie didn't know who the sportswriter was talking about. Then it came to him, the name of the man who once played center field in Seals Stadium. Why, it was none other than Willie's boyhood idol, Joe DiMaggio!

"But that's silly," Willie said. "Joe hasn't played in years."

"That's right," the sportswriter answered. "But in this town he is still the greatest."

"He's the greatest in my book, too," Willie said. "I don't want to take his place. I just want to be accepted for what I am."

"Then just keep on playing like Willie Mays," the sportswriter said. "Sooner or later the fans will all be on your side."

Willie took the advice. A few days later he went on a home-run streak. Between April 26 and May 23, he hit thirteen home runs — seven of them against the Dodgers. There were fewer boos now, but the fans' favorite was not Willie Mays; it was the rookie first baseman who followed him in the line-up, Orlando Cepeda.

Even if San Francisco didn't take to player Willie Mays, Willie Mays certainly took to playing in San Francisco. He rapped out 208 hits for a batting average of .347, just missing the National League batting championship. He also hit 29 home runs and led the league in stolen bases with 31. More than any other player on the team, Willie was responsible for the Giants' finishing a strong third that year.

Even so, when a San Francisco newspaper took a public poll to find the Giants' most valuable player, Orlando Cepeda won easily. Willie wasn't upset when he read the results. Cepeda had had an excellent season. He had hit .312 and batted in ninety-six runs — the same number as Willie.

The Giants came up with another fine rookie in 1959, a tall, rangy first baseman named Willie McCovey, and it looked for a time as though they might capture a National League pennant in their second season in San Francisco. Willie Mays enjoyed another fine season, hitting .313 with 34 home runs and 104 runs batted in. He also led the league in base-stealing for the fourth straight year with 27.

The All-Star Game of that year was played in Pittsburgh, and Willie made some spectacular catches before winning the game with a tremendous triple to center field. "The only man who could have caught it," wrote one of the reporters covering the game, "hit it."

All during that 1959 season, the Giants and Dodgers fought it out for the championship. When the teams opened their last series of the season late in September, the Giants led by two games. Then disaster struck. The Dodgers won all three games of the series, and the Giants dropped all the way to third place, a game behind the Dodgers, and a half-game behind the surging Milwaukee Braves.

The pennant race went right down to the last day of the season, when the Giants lost a double-header to the St. Louis Cardinals and finished third. (The Dodgers and Braves finished in a first-place tie, and had a play-off against each other before the Dodgers won the right to go into the World Series.)

The Giants were bitterly disappointed, and so were their new San Francisco fans. Some of the fans were unfair. They blamed Willie for the failure of the Giants to finish in first place.

"He should have bunted more to get on base," many said. "He shouldn't have been trying for home runs all the time."

Willie's comment was, "I'll bunt when the situation calls for it. But I'm supposed to be a hitter, not a bunter."

"Well, you're making progress, Willie,"

said one of his teammates. "First they wanted you to hit homers every time you came to bat. Now, they want bunts instead."

"I sure can't win," said Willie sadly.

But by the time the 1960 season started, Willie was beginning to feel more like his old cheerful self. For one thing, he had found a house in San Francisco. Also, Horace Stoneham had given him a contract for $85,-000, making Willie the highest-paid player in baseball that year. Finally, Willie was looking forward to playing in Candlestick Park, the brand-new stadium which the city had built especially for the Giants.

Then, sometime just before the season opened, Willie heard about the wind at Candlestick Park. San Francisco is a breezy city, and Willie had gotten used to the way the wind could carry a fly ball at Seals Stadium. But Candlestick Park, more exposed to the winds that blew off San Francisco Bay, was a different story. Even the stadium architect was quoted as saying: "Willie Mays will need all the talent he has to run down some of the balls that will fly out there, twisting and turning in the wind."

When Willie saw the new stadium for the first time, he was amazed at how the wind blew from left field toward right-center field. A well-hit ball to left field seemed to hesitate in mid-air, then drift sideways. Not only was it hard to hit a ball well into the outfield, but it was even more difficult to catch one out there. Willie quickly learned to keep an eye on the ball at all times before making a catch. Occasionally he ran so far to catch a ball that he found himself in the territory normally covered by the right fielder or the second baseman.

In 1960 most experts picked the Giants to win the National League pennant. The team started off the season well, but soon it was plain that the Pittsburgh Pirates were just a little better. The Giants couldn't seem to get by Pittsburgh, and they fell farther behind in June, when the Pirates swept a three-game series against them at Candlestick Park. The disappointed fans booed their own team.

Willie was sitting in the dressing room after the third defeat, feeling terrible, when one of the other players came over and said quietly, "Did you hear? They just fired Rig."

At first Willie couldn't believe it. Why would the Giants want to fire manager Bill Rigney in the middle of the season, with the team in second place? But it was true. Stone-

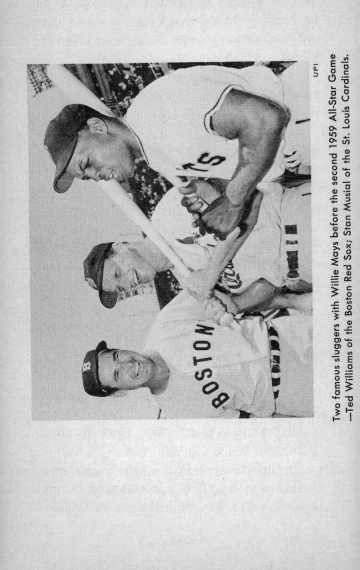

Two famous sluggers with Willie Mays before the second 1959 All-Star Game —Ted Williams of the Boston Red Sox; Stan Musial of the St. Louis Cardinals.

ham had decided that a new manager would have a better chance to lead the Giants to victory. He had named Tom Sheehan to finish the 1960 season while he looked for the right man.

Sheehan was a sixty-six-year-old former pitcher, who had spent most of his dozen years with the Giants as a scout. All of the players knew him and liked him, but few of them could take him seriously as a manager. After all, he was only filling in until the end of the season. And without a strong manager, the Giants dropped to fifth place.

The only Giants' player to hit over .300 that season was Willie Mays. He finished with 190 hits, including 29 home runs and a .319 average. The boos, when he came to bat, were getting harder to hear in a growing chorus of cheers.

Before the 1961 season, the Giants made two changes that were to have a great effect on Willie. They shortened the fences at Candlestick Park so that the longest distance for a home run was 410 feet to center field. And they hired Alvin Dark as their manager.

The new fences made it easier to hit home runs, and in 1961 Willie proved it by hitting twenty-one of his forty homers in Candlestick Park. He had hit only twelve there the year before.

But the new manager was even more important to Willie. Alvin Dark had been a player with Willie on the old New York Giants, and Willie had liked him. Two days after Dark was named manager, he sent this message to Willie: "Knowing you will be playing for me is the greatest privilege and thrill any manager could ever hope to have."

The note was only the first shot in a campaign that Dark had decided to wage to convince both Willie and the people of San Francisco that he was a great player. All that spring and right into the 1961 season, Dark went out of his way to tell everyone what an outstanding player Willie Mays was. He said, on a radio show, "Without Willie Mays, the Giants are an ordinary ball club."

For a while, at the beginning of the season, it looked as though Dark's efforts weren't going to pay off. Willie got off to a very poor start. He was hitting only .250 and had failed to get a hit in seven straight times at bat. On top of that, he got sick in Milwaukee.

Willie was rooming with Willie McCovey, who had hit a pair of home runs one afternoon. Late that night in their hotel room,

McCovey decided to celebrate with a midnight snack and he ordered two portions of spareribs, a favorite treat for both players.

Not too long after eating, Willie felt a sharp pain in his stomach. It got worse as he tossed on his bed, unable to sleep, and finally he reached for the telephone and called Doc Bowman, the team trainer. Bowman, still in his pajamas, hurried to Willie's room, and gave him some pills and medicine for his stomach. Finally Willie was able to get some sleep. But he felt very weak the next morning when he arrived at the ball park to get ready for the afternoon game with the Braves.

He told Dark what had happened and said, "I'm not sure I can play today."

"Take a few swings in batting practice," Dark replied. "See how you feel then."

Willie began to feel a little better as he stood in the batting cage. He was able to hit the ball all right, and when he finished his swings, he walked over to the manager and said simply, "I'll play."

What happened that day made baseball history. Willie got up in the first inning and drove one of Lew Burdette's fast balls 420 feet for a home run. He did it again in the third inning, hitting the ball 400 feet. In the fifth inning, he was out on a sharp line drive to center field, but in the sixth inning he hit a ball 450 feet for his third home run of the game. In the eighth inning he drove a pitch by Don McMahon 430 feet for another homer. He had become the ninth man in baseball history to hit four home runs in one game!

In the ninth inning, Willie was the next batter due up when the Braves' pitcher got the third out to end the game. The Braves' fans actually booed as the out was made, for they wanted to see if Willie could be the first man ever to hit five home runs in a game.

The final score was 14–4, and Willie had personally accounted for eight of the Giants' runs. In the dressing room, when reporters asked him if he might have hit a fifth home run, Willie grinned and answered, "I suppose so. I sure would have liked to try it. Can you imagine what the odds would have been against me?"

The four home runs cured Willie's stomach trouble and his slump at the same time. Base hits began coming off his bat the way they always had, and Willie's batting average shot upward. But as great as that afternoon in Milwaukee was, Willie had a day just

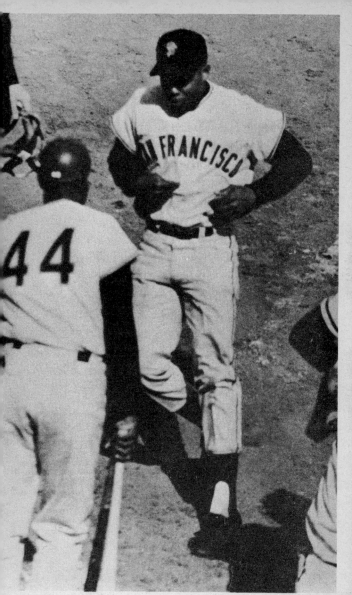

Willie Mays jogs into home plate and becomes the ninth man in baseball history to hit four home runs in one game.

two months later that in some ways was even greater.

It was on June 29, 1961, the day after a night game between the Giants and the Philadelphia Phillies. The teams had battled for five hours and eleven minutes to a 7–7 tie in fifteen innings before the game was finally called. A double-header was scheduled for the next day, and Willie was one weary player when he arrived at the field.

Nevertheless, the Giants proceeded to win both games as Willie demolished the Phillies almost singlehanded. In the first game he got four hits — including three home runs — and drove in five runs in an 8–7 victory. In the second game, he doubled and tripled to drive in two runs, and broke up a Phillies' rally by throwing a runner out at home plate, as the Giants won 4–1.

Willie had a third great day in 1961. That was when the Giants returned to New York to play an exhibition game with the Yankees at Yankee Stadium. The Giants weren't sure what sort of reception they would get from the New York fans they had left behind. But they soon found out.

It was raining hard when the Giants arrived at Yankee Stadium. The pregame practice was canceled and the game was delayed. But when the Giants finally got out on the field, they were greeted by a near-capacity crowd of 50,000. Most of the fans had sat waiting patiently in the rain for nearly an hour.

Now, the crowd hushed as the announcer read the names of the Giants' starters. "At second base, number fourteen, Joe Amalfitano," the voice boomed over the public address system. There was a cheer.

"In right field, number seven, Harvey Kuenn," came the voice, and the applause grew louder.

"In center field, number twenty-four, Wil — "

The rest was drowned out as the great crowd stood and roared for Willie Mays. For over a minute, the sound bounced all over the stadium, so loud that it could even be heard in the darkened Polo Grounds just across the Harlem River. The sound was doubly sweet to Willie. He hadn't heard that kind of wild enthusiasm for himself in a long time, and it sent a tingle up and down his spine.

The Giants tried hard to win the pennant for Alvin Dark in 1961, and nobody tried harder than Willie Mays. But they gradually dropped to third place and finished eight games behind first-place Cincinnati. Willie hit .308 with 40 home runs and 123 runs batted in.

"You had another good year, Willie," a friend said to him shortly after the season ended.

"It wasn't bad," Willie replied, "but I just wish I could play for one more pennant winner."

"Wait till next year," said his friend, using an old Dodgers' slogan.

Willie smiled. "That could be the year, all right," he said.

12

Hero of Candlestick Park at Last

WILLIE MAYS couldn't remember ever being as tired as he was now, in the final days of the 1962 season. To one reporter who asked him how he felt, Willie just sighed and said, "I'll be awful glad when it's all over."

There were two reasons why Willie had played himself into exhaustion in 1962. The first was that the Giants again were locked in a tight pennant race. That alone put a lot of pressure on Willie because he always wanted to help his team as much as he could. The second reason was the break-up of Willie's marriage.

His wife hadn't been happy in San Francisco. She wanted to live in New York City. Willie tried to keep her happy by buying two homes, one in San Francisco and one in New Rochelle, a suburb of New York City. During the season, Willie and his wife lived in the San Francisco home. As soon as the season was over they moved to New Rochelle.

But it didn't work, and finally Willie and his wife agreed that it might be best for them to separate. The divorce upset Willie very much, especially as his small, adopted son Michael went with his mother. To keep from thinking about his family problems, Willie played harder than ever.

The result was an outstanding season for Willie. He hit .304, a few points lower than he had in 1961, but his 49 home runs and 141 runs batted in were considerably more than he had hit the year before. All season long, Willie smashed hits, made dazzling catches, and ran the bases fearlessly as the Giants and the Dodgers battled it out for the pennant.

The Giants had cut the Dodgers' lead to a mere half-game by mid-September, when the team left San Francisco for its last road trip. Willie had begun to notice how tired he was after every game, but he didn't pay much attention to it. He tried to get a few extra hours of sleep, and by the next day he usually felt all right.

Then, one hot and muggy night in Cincinnati, Willie *didn't* feel all right. It was only the beginning of the second inning, and already he felt as tired as if he had played an entire double-header. He was sitting in the dugout at Crosley Field, when suddenly everything seemed to spin before his eyes and he passed out.

When he opened his eyes again, he saw the worried face of trainer Doc Bowman bending over him. "It's all right, Willie," the trainer assured him. "How do you feel?"

"I just feel like I don't want to move," Willie replied. "I can move, but I'd rather not."

"Get a stretcher!" Doc Bowman yelled at a couple of players who stood nearby.

They carried Willie to the dressing room, and then took him to the hospital in an ambulance. Willie was scared. He'd had dizzy spells before, but he'd never passed out. He felt a little better, however, when the doctor finished his tests and came to his bed.

"There's nothing wrong with you, Willie," he said. "But you're just run down physically. You need a rest."

"But for how long, doctor?" Willie asked. "When can I play again."

"That's up to you," the doctor said. "I certainly think you should rest for a few days."

Alvin Dark agreed with the doctor's opinion, and he announced to the newspapers that "Mays will play again when he says he's ready."

Up to the moment of Willie's collapse, the Giants had won seven games in a row. But now, with Willie out of the line-up, they proceeded to lose four straight games, then two more when Willie first returned. By the time the Giants got back to San Francisco, they were four games behind the Dodgers with only seven games left to play. Though Willie was active again, it seemed impossible for the Giants to catch up.

Fortunately the Dodgers were stumbling badly, and on the last day of the season only one game separated them from the second-place Giants. The Giants played Houston on that final day, and the score was tied 1–1 in the eighth inning when Willie came to bat and hit a tremendous 450-foot blast off pitcher Dick Farrell. That long home run won the game for the Giants. Meanwhile, the Dodgers were losing their last game to the St. Louis Cardinals, and the pennant race finished in a tie. There would have to be a play-off.

In the first game of the best-of-three-game play-off series, the Giants blasted the sore-armed Dodger ace, Sandy Koufax. Willie led the attack with two home runs as the Giants won 8–0. But the next day the Giants blew a five-run lead and lost the game to even the series.

The third and final game was to be played in Los Angeles on October 3rd. Willie didn't have to be reminded that eleven years ago to the very day Bobby Thomson had won another play-off series with the Dodgers.

As the game wore on, it seemed as though history was repeating itself. For the Dodgers were leading 4–2 as the Giants got ready for their last turn at bat in the top of the ninth inning.

The pitcher was the first man scheduled to bat, and Manager Dark sent up Matty Alou to pinch-hit. Alou promptly singled. Leadoff hitter Harvey Kuenn was up next, but the best he could do was a ground ball on which the Dodgers were able to force out Alou at second base. Then Willie McCovey was sent up to pinch-hit for Chuck Hiller and drew a base on balls. That brought up Felipe Alou, Matty's brother, and Willie watched closely from the on-deck circle as Dodger relief pitcher Ed Roebuck walked Felipe to fill the bases.

As Willie strode to the plate, he could hear

the Dodgers' fans murmuring. On the pitcher's mound, a little group of Dodger players gathered to decide how to handle the critical situation. Willie felt certain they would try to pitch low to him to prevent a grand-slam home run. But that didn't worry him. He felt sure he could get a single and drive in the tying runs, and that was exactly what he tried to do.

He timed his swing perfectly, and smashed the ball right back to the pitcher's mound. The ball caromed off Roebuck's leg into center field for a single that scored Kuenn from third base. But the slower McCovey was held at third, and the bases remained loaded.

Willie's hit had done more than score a run. It had forced the Dodgers to take out Roebuck and put in Stan Williams, a tired pitcher who had won the day before. Williams pitched to Orlando Cepeda who hit a fly ball that allowed McCovey to score the tying run. Before the Dodgers got the third out, two bases on balls and an error had allowed two more runs to score and the Giants led 6–4.

When relief pitcher Billy Pierce set the Dodgers down in order in the last of the ninth, the Giants had once more snatched a pennant from the Dodgers. The last out came

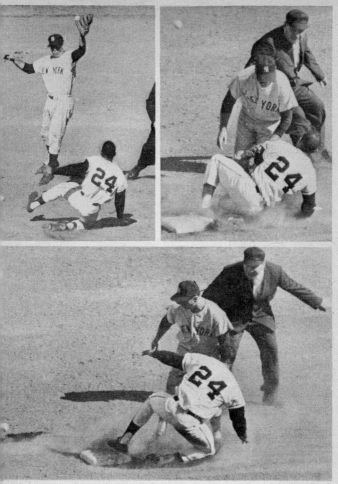

Mays steals second base as Yankee Bobbie Richardson loses
the ball during the sixth game of the 1962 World Series.

on a soft line drive to center field that Willie raced under and caught. As the umpire gave the *out* sign, Willie leaped high in the air, threw the ball into the stands, then raced to the Giants' dugout, where his teammates were slapping and hugging each other in their joy.

The Giants' clubhouse was so full of reporters, television cameramen, and well-wishers that Willie could hardly find his way to his locker. It was like the old days at the Polo Grounds as the players yelled happily to each other and people kept coming over to say, "Nice going, Willie," "Good game, Buck," or just "We did it!"

When the team finally boarded the plane for the ride back to San Francisco, there was another surprise. Over the intercom came the captain's voice, announcing that there would be a delay in landing because Giants' fans were swarming over the airport and even dashing across the runways.

As the plane landed, and the players trooped down the steps, Willie saw a sight he had never expected to see in San Francisco. The fences were lined with a solid wall of people, some 30,000 of them, cheering each one of the players. And the loudest cheers of all were for Willie Mays. The last words Willie heard as the team bus left the airport was the chant, "We want Mays! We want Mays!"

It was an awfully good sound.

The San Francisco fans were so happy and proud of their team that they didn't even mind the Giants' losing the World Series to the favored New York Yankees.

In 1963 Willie Mays was hitting well under .300 for most of the season. Some people said he was getting old and losing his skill. But Willie didn't agree, even though he was thirty-two years old in May.

A few days before his birthday (May 6th), the Giants returned to the old New York Polo Grounds, which had not yet been torn down, to play a year-old team, the New York Mets. It still seemed a little strange to Willie to be going into the visitor's clubhouse at the old ball park, instead of the home clubhouse. But Willie was no stranger to the fans who now cheered for the Mets.

May 3rd was Willie Mays Night at the Polo Grounds, and Willie received a standing ovation from the 50,000 fans who were there. They cheered and cheered before the game, as Willie accepted a gold key to the city and loads of gifts (most of which he

Cheering fans flock to the Polo Grounds on May 3rd, 1963, to celebrate Willie Mays Day. They were also cheering their new home team, the New York Mets.

later donated to the city's Police Athletic League). Old teammates like Monte Irvin and Bobby Thomson came over to shake Willie's hand and congratulate him.

"I really and truly appreciate this night," Willie said, when the pregame ceremonies were over. "I feel this is my home."

To show how much he felt at home, Willie put on one of his typical performances for the New York crowd. In the first inning, he made a head-first slide into first base trying to beat out a hit. In the third inning, he got a single and suddenly turned and dashed safely to second when he noticed the outfielder taking his time about throwing the ball back. Later in the game, he made a long run into right-center field to take an extra-base hit away from the Mets' Ron Hunt.

After the game, the other players teased Willie about the honors he had received. But the teasing stopped when an attendant handed Willie a telegram that read:

"I would like to join the many loyal fans at the Polo Grounds tonight honoring your achievements in the world of baseball. This honor is well deserved and I know we can look forward to many years of the exciting spectacle of Willie Mays at bat and in the field."

It was signed — John F. Kennedy.

But a few weeks later, Willie was beginning to wonder whether he was letting the President and all his fans down. He had always hit in streaks, but now the streaks would not come. Instead there were long periods when Willie couldn't even get a hit. By July, with the season half over, he was hitting only .236. Then, quite suddenly, he caught fire.

It began on July 21st at Cincinnati. Willie lashed out two hits to lead the Giants to victory, and began a hitting streak that was to make up for the hits he had missed earlier. On July 23rd he hit two home runs to beat the Mets. The next day he scored the winning run against them by walking, stealing third base, and sliding home safely after a short fly ball was caught. The day after that, he beat the Mets again with three hits and a great shoe-top catch that saved two runs. And so it went, day after day, as his batting average inched steadily upward. On August 27th, shortly after he had finally reached the .300 mark in the 1963 season, Willie blasted the 400th home run of his career off Cardinal pitcher Curt Simmons.

When the writers came into the clubhouse to interview him after that game, one of them asked, "Willie, when you were doing so badly early in the season, were you worried?"

The big grin filled Willie's face and he shouted, "*I* wasn't worried. It was you writers who were worried!"

But to his friends Willie confessed that the streak had taken a lot out of him, and that he was feeling just as tired as he had at the end of the 1962 season. And a few days later the whole baseball world found out how exhausted Willie Mays really was.

The Giants were playing the Chicago Cubs at Candlestick Park, and Willie came to bat in the fourth inning with the bases loaded. He took a cut at the first pitch and fouled it off. But as he finished his swing, he began to get the same dizzy feeling that he had had the year before in Cincinnati. Quickly he dropped to one knee while the umpire and catcher stared at him. In a moment Doc Bowman was at his side with smelling salts, and Willie was able to get up and walk slowly back to the dugout as the crowd buzzed in disbelief. Once again, Willie was sent to the hospital, given a complete check-up, and ordered to rest for several days.

Though Willie didn't play for a few days, when the season was finally over, he had a .314 batting average — his best in three seasons — with 38 home runs and 103 runs batted in to his credit.

The 1964 season was like 1963 — but in reverse. This time Willie was playing well right from the start. He ran up a twenty-game hitting streak while hitting safely in twenty-four of his first twenty-seven games. For the month of April, his batting average was an incredible .489.

During this amazing streak, Juan Marichal, the Giants' ace pitcher, was scheduled to pitch a game in Houston. Before the game started, Marichal stormed up to Willie, making believe he was very angry. "You didn't hit any homers the last time I pitched," he yelled, "so you owe me two!"

"Have a heart, Juan," Willie complained, trying to keep from laughing, "This is a big ball park."

But he went out and hit two home runs — and a single for good measure — to help Marichal to an easy 6–0 victory.

As the season wore on, though, Willie began to feel tired again. He couldn't seem to get as many base hits, but he could still steal bases and make his famous sensational catches. One of these catches is still rated among his greatest.

It came in August against the Dodgers in

Los Angeles. In the first inning, Willie, while running at top speed, had made a sensational knee-high catch of a drive by Ron Fairly. But that catch was all but forgotten after his feat in the eighth inning.

The Dodgers' Willie Davis hit a ball that seemed certain to go for extra bases. It was into right-center field and curving away from Willie Mays, who took off toward right field. No one expected him to catch up to it, but suddenly Willie leaped into the air, thrust his glove out as far as his arm could reach, and managed to grab the ball. His throw to first base almost produced a double play as Fairly, who was on his way to third base when Willie caught the ball, barely got back in time.

When Willie trotted in from the outfield at the end of the inning, the 36,000 Dodger fans stood and applauded the rival star. Willie tipped his cap and grinned happily.

Willie hit only .205 in September, however, and this cost him a chance to finish over .300 for the season. When Willie's average dropped to .296 — his lowest in eight seasons — some writers questioned whether Willie, at the age of thirty-three, would ever be able to hit .300 again. They also wondered how much longer Willie Mays could play.

13

"He Can Still Do It All"

"SURE, I'm getting older," said Willie as he prepared to leave for the Phoenix training camp in 1965. "I've thought about retiring, too. But I think I can still play the way I always have. I may need more rest, but I'm going to keep going until I feel I'm embarrassing myself. When that time comes, I don't want to keep on playing."

"When do you think that will be?" a reporter asked Willie.

Willie's eyes twinkled and he tried his best to keep from laughing as he answered, "Maybe when I'm forty — or forty-five."

In 1965 thirty-four-year-old Willie Mays proceeded to amaze the people who said he was getting too old. For that year Willie had one of the best seasons of his long career, topping it off by winning the Most Valuable Player award for the second time.

Willie's spectacular performance was partly due to the new atmosphere on the Giants' team. Alvin Dark had been released as manager after the 1964 season and replaced by Herman Franks, who had been a Giants' coach for many years. Although Willie had gotten along well with Dark, some of the other players had resented his strictness. Franks was more easy-going and he got along well with all the players. There was laughter and joking in the Giants' clubhouse, and Willie felt more relaxed and happy than he had in a long time.

Franks had been ordered to rebuild the team with several new players, so nobody expected the Giants to be a serious pennant contender in 1965. But with Willie hitting in his old-time style, the Giants suddenly found themselves right in the thick of the pennant race. They didn't quite make it, but it was no fault of Willie's. He hit fifty-two home runs that season to lead the National League and set a new Giants' record, and the seventeen homers that he stroked in the month of August set a new major-league record.

On September 13, 1965, with the Giants fighting the Dodgers for first place, Willie stepped to the plate in Houston and hit one of Don Nottebart's fast balls into the center-field seats. Suddenly the Houston scoreboard lit up with a huge "500." The fans, who needed no one to explain that it was the 500th home run of Willie's career, stood and applauded wildly. So did the rest of the Giants who clustered around Willie as he crossed home plate.

One of the players waiting to congratulate him was veteran pitcher Warren Spahn, who had been obtained by the Giants from the Mets earlier that season.

"How about that, Willie," he said. "I saw your first one and now I've seen your five hundredth."

"Same pitch, too," Willie said.

"Oh no," said Spahn. "I threw you a curve back in '51."

"It wasn't a curve," insisted Willie. "It was a fast ball."

They argued good-naturedly about it, and when Spahn walked off, Willie admitted to another teammate, "You know, maybe it was a curve. Pitchers remember that sort of thing longer than hitters."

Willie finished with a .317 average that season, but he was quite surprised when it was announced that he had again won the

Willie blasts his 511th home run, tying Mel Ott's record as the greatest home-run hitter in National League history.

Valuable Player award, beating out Dodgers' pitcher Sandy Koufax.

"It's been eleven years since I won my first one," Willie said to a friend. "I guess old age agrees with me."

With Willie approaching his thirty-fifth birthday in 1966, however, there was more talk about how much longer he could play. One reporter noted that Willie had played in 157 of the Giants' 163 games in 1965, and even Willie had to admit that was a lot of games.

The Giants decided to do everything they could to make sure Willie got more rest. They even went so far as to pick up a player, Don Landrum, from the Chicago Cubs just to fill in for Willie in the second game of double-headers and during the late innings of un-important games.

Willie proceeded to hit .383 in spring exhibition games, which led his old boss, Leo Durocher, to remark, "Willie will be playing better than anybody else when he's in a rocking chair."

The 1966 season was barely under way in April when Willie blasted his 511th home run off Jim Owens of Houston and moved into a tie with Mel Ott as the greatest home-run hitter in National League history. Afterward Willie tried to pretend it was nothing important. When a reporter asked him what was going through his mind as he circled the bases, Willie answered, "I was thinking it's a tied ball game, and we have a chance to win it."

But Willie was deeply touched when a cake was rolled in. On it was written "Say Hey, 511." Then Franks handed him a baseball autographed by all the other members of the team. "It's the one you hit," said Franks. "I had to pay a guy fifty bucks for it, but it was worth it."

But now came the worst time for Willie. Everyone was waiting for him to hit number 512 and break Ott's record, and Willie began to feel the pressure. Instead of swinging for base hits, he found himself swinging for home runs — and getting nothing. In his next twenty-three times at bat, he managed only three hits, none of them homers.

Finally, on May 4, at exactly 9:08 p.m., Willie Mays passed Ott's record and became the leading home-run hitter in National League history. The Giants were playing the Dodgers at Candlestick Park. Willie took a shot at a high, outside change-up thrown by Claude Osteen and hit it over the right-field fence. The crowd roared for over five minutes. Willie had to keep popping out of the dugout and waving his cap. Even then, the crowd kept yelling, "We want Willie!" over and over again.

The milestones came up regularly after that. On June 23rd, Willie hit number 521 at Chicago to tie Ted Williams for third place on the list of the greatest home-run hitters in major-league history. But he drew a bigger hand from the Cubs' fans that day when he plucked a long drive by Ernie Banks out of the vines that cover the center-field wall at Wrigley Field.

On August 16th, Willie tied Jimmy Foxx for the second spot on the home-run list by hitting number 534 off the Cardinals' Al Jackson. The very next day, Willie hit a three-and-two pitch by the Cardinals' Ray Washburn over the right-field fence to pass Foxx. Only the great Babe Ruth, with 714 home runs, had ever hit more than Willie.

But Willie was doing much more than simply hitting home runs in 1966. He was playing the kind of baseball that much younger men could only marvel at. There was, for example, the game that the Giants played against the Dodgers at Los Angeles early in September. Although Willie didn't hit a home run that time, he personally led the Giants to a 3–2 victory in twelve innings.

He walked in the first inning and scored ahead of Jim Hart's home run. In the eighth inning, he made a spectacular ankle-high catch of a drive hit by Tommy Davis to save what would have been the winning Dodger run. Finally, in the twelfth inning, with two out and nobody on base, he worked Dodger pitcher Joe Moeller for a base on balls. When rookie Frank Johnson singled, Willie was already on his way to second base. He kept going to third, made a big turn toward home and, when the second baseman hesitated in throwing to the plate, Willie kept right on running. The ball reached catcher John Roseboro before Willie did, but Willie slid in hard and kicked the ball out of Roseboro's mitt to score the winning run.

Altogether, Willie played in 152 games in 1966, hitting .288, with 37 home runs. Although it was a good season, it was quite a drop-off from his 1965 performance.

As the 1967 season began, even Willie himself was beginning to wonder if the years had caught up with him at last. There was the day, for example, when he was struck out four times in one game by pitcher Gary Nolan of Cincinnati.

At top speed, Mays races fifty yards to catch Cub Ron Hunt-
ley's long fly. Teammate Ollie Brown cuts out of the way.

"These kid pitchers," sighed Willie. "They're all so big and strong and throw the ball so hard, they make you feel old too soon."

In July Willie came down with a bad case of flu. He returned to the line-up a short time later, but he felt weak for the rest of the season. At about this time the Giants opened a series in Atlanta, and Willie found himself in a very unusual situation — for him.

In the third inning, with the Giants leading 1–0 and two men on base, the Braves' manager Billy Hitchcock did something that no manager had ever dared to do before. He ordered Jim Hart walked intentionally so that his pitcher could face Willie Mays with the bases loaded!

"Hart was their hottest hitter," Hitchcock explained later, "while Mays hadn't driven in a run in two weeks. The move made sense."

It made sense until Willie swung on a two-strike pitch and hit a single just beyond first base to drive in what proved to be the winning run.

But Willie didn't get too many hits like that one. Over the season he averaged only .263, with 22 home runs and 70 runs batted in. It wasn't a bad record for most ball-players, but it was the worst of Willie's career.

"No, I won't quit if I have another bad year," he told an interviewer, giving him the broad Mays grin. "Furthermore, I'm not planning on having another bad year."

Willie started the 1968 season as though he meant what he had said. He got eight hits in his first seventeen times at bat and was among the league leaders on May 6 when the Giants visited Houston. The Astros' owner, Roy Hofheinz, decided that since it was Willie's thirty-seventh birthday, he should have a birthday cake. And what a birthday cake it was! It took 3,800 eggs, 150 pounds of sugar, 150 pounds of butter, 300 pounds of flour, and 100 pounds of nuts to produce a cake that weighed exactly 569 pounds — one pound for every Willie Mays home run.

Willie posed for pictures beside the cake, cut off a few slices for his teammates, and then asked that the rest of the huge cake be sent to a local children's hospital.

In July Willie was named to the National League All-Star team for the nineteenth time. This time, Willie was supposed to be a late-inning substitute. But when starting outfielder Pete Rose of Cincinnati broke his thumb, Willie started in his place and scored the only run of the game in the first inning.

It was a typical Mays effort. Hitting against Cleveland's Luis Tiant, Willie singled and went to second base when Tiant threw wildly on a pick-off attempt. Then he worried Tiant into a wild pitch to get to third base and scurried home on a double-play. For this bit of base running, Mays was named the game's most valuable player.

Willie had said that he didn't plan to have a bad year, and he didn't. He got 144 hits for a .289 batting average that included 79 runs batted in and 23 home runs.

Willie finished the 1968 season with 587 home runs, and the countdown to 600 began with the opening of the 1969 season. It was to be a slow countdown, however, for at the age of thirty-eight Willie needed more rest than ever. He was also slowed down by a painful knee injury that hurt him most of the year. He didn't hit number 598 until August 17th, and then there was a wait of almost a month until he hit number 599 on September 12th.

There were only fifteen games left in the season and everyone hoped that Willie would hit number 600 during a series with the Dodgers in San Francisco. But Willie wasn't able to connect in any of the three games. The new Giants' manager, Clyde King, decided to rest Willie the next night, in the opening game of a series at San Diego. But when the score was tied at 2–2 in the seventh inning and the Giants needed a pinch-hitter, King turned to his bench.

"Willie, grab a bat," he said.

Willie grabbed a bat and went to the plate to face rookie pitcher Mike Corkins. There was a Giant runner on base and all that Willie wanted to do was get a hit that would score the runner, or at least move him up a base. Instead, he swung at a fast ball around his knees and hit it down the left-field line and out of the park for the historic 600th home run. The small crowd in San Diego cheered and all of the Giants swarmed out of their dugout to greet Willie at home plate and escort him back to the bench.

"It sure was a long time coming," said Willie after the game. "There were times when I wondered if I was ever going to hit it. But the big thing isn't that it was number 600. The big thing is that it won the game."

Winning the game has always been the most important thing for Willie Mays, from his childhood days in Alabama through his

Willie Mays of the New York Mets watches the flight of the ball as he hits a game-winning home run on May 14, 1972, against his former team, the San Francisco Giants. Greeted by a standing ovation in his first game as a Met, Mays repaid the tribute by hitting his 647th career home run, which proved to be the margin in the game as New York won 5-4.

brilliant career with the San Francisco Giants and now with the New York Mets. And yet, when he finally retires, Willie will leave behind one of the greatest baseball records in the history of the game.

But retirement isn't on Mays' mind just yet. Returning to New York, where he first broke into the majors, was a great thrill for Willie. "I'm so glad to be back that I know it'll add a lot of spark to my game, even at my age," he said. (Willie will be 42 on his next birthday.)

"Willie will really help us," said manager Yogi Berra. "There are still a lot of hits left in that bat of his, and I know a lot of his spirit will rub off on our other guys."

Shortly after Willie was named to the team of baseball's Greatest Living Players in 1969, Leo Durocher talked about the man he had brought to the major leagues.

"He could pick up a team and carry it on his back," Durocher said. "Maybe it was a hit, maybe it was a catch, maybe it was the way he ran the bases. Every day he came to play. Every day he'd do the unexpected."

"But Leo," one of his listeners interrupted. "You're talking about Willie when he was in his twenties. He's old now and he gets tired."

"I know that," said Durocher. "But he still can do it all whenever he wants to. Even today, this minute, he's more exciting than anybody who ever played this game."

WILLIE MAYS' RECORD

Born on May 6, 1931, in Westfield, Alabama. Resides in Atherton, California. Height, 5:11. Weight, 187 pounds. Bats right. Throws right.

Year	Club	Pos	G	AB	R	H	2B	3B	HR	RBI	BB	SO	BA
1950	Trenton	OF	81	306	50	108	20	8	4	55	42	34	.353
1951	Minneapolis	OF	35	149	38	71	18	3	8	30	14	10	.477
1951	New York	OF	121	464	59	127	22	5	20	68	56	60	.274
1952	New York+	OF	34	127	17	30	2	4	4	23	16	17	.236
1953	New York					(in Military Service)							
1954	New York	OF	151	565	119	195	33	*13	41	110	66	57	*.345
1955	New York	OF	152	580	123	185	18	•13	*51	127	79	60	.319
1956	New York	OF	152	578	101	171	27	8	36	84	68	65	.296
1957	New York	OF	152	585	112	195	26	*20	35	97	76	62	.333
1958	San Fran.	OF	152	600	*121	208	33	11	29	96	78	56	.347
1959	San Fran.	OF	151	575	125	180	43	5	34	104	65	58	.313
1960	San Fran.	OF	153	595	107	*190	29	12	29	103	61	70	.319
1961	San Fran.	OF	154	572	*129	176	32	3	40	123	81	77	.308
1962	San Fran.	OF	162	621	130	189	36	5	*49	141	78	85	.304
1963	San Fran.	OF-SS	157	596	115	187	32	7	38	103	66	83	.314
1964	San Fran.	OF-IF	157	578	121	171	21	9	*47	111	82	72	.296
1965	San Fran.	OF	152	558	118	177	21	3	*52	112	76	71	.317
1966	San Fran.	OF	152	552	99	159	29	4	37	103	70	81	.288
1967	San Fran.	OF	141	486	83	128	22	2	22	70	51	92	.263
1968	San Fran.	OF-1B	148	498	84	144	20	5	23	79	67	81	.289
1969	San Fran.	OF	117	403	64	114	17	3	13	58	49	71	.283
1970	San Fran.	OF-1B	139	478	94	139	15	2	28	83	79	90	.291
1971	San Fran.	OF-1B	136	417	82	113	24	5	18	61	112	123	.271
Major-League Totals			2838	10,428	2003	3178	502	139	646	1856	1376	1431	.305

+ — Entered military service May 29.
* — Denotes led league.
• — Tied for league lead.

World Series Record

Year	Club	Pos	G	AB	R	H	2B	3B	HR	RBI	BB	SO	BA
1951	New York	OF	6	22	1	4	0	0	0	1	2	2	.182
1954	New York	OF	4	14	4	4	1	0	0	3	4	1	.286
1962	San Francisco	OF	7	28	3	7	2	0	0	1	1	5	.250
World Series Totals			17	64	8	15	3	0	0	5	7	8	.234

All-Star Game Record

Year	Club	Pos	G	AB	R	H	2B	3B	HR	RBI	BB	SO	BA
1954	National	OF	1	2	1	1	0	0	0	0	0	0	.500
1955	National	OF	1	3	2	2	0	0	0	0	0	1	.667
1956	National	OF	1	3	2	1	0	0	1	2	1	2	.333
1957	National	OF	1	4	2	2	0	1	0	1	0	1	.500
1958	National	OF	1	4	2	1	0	0	0	0	0	0	.250
1959	National	OF	2	8	0	1	0	0	1	0	1	1	.125
1960	National	OF	2	8	2	6	1	1	1	1	0	0	.750
1961	National	OF	2	8	2	3	1	0	0	1	1	1	.375
1962	National	OF	2	5	0	2	0	0	0	0	1	0	.400
1963	National	OF	1	3	2	1	0	0	0	2	1	1	.333
1964	National	OF	1	3	1	0	0	0	0	0	1	0	.000
1965	National	OF	1	3	2	1	0	0	1	1	2	1	.333
1966	National	OF	1	4	1	1	0	0	0	0	0	1	.250
1967	National	OF	1	4	0	0	0	0	0	0	0	1	.000
1968	National	OF	1	4	1	1	0	0	0	0	0	1	.250
1969	National	PH	1	1	0	0	0	0	0	0	0	0	.000
1970	National	OF	1	3	0	0	0	0	0	0	0	0	.000
1971	National	OF	1	2	0	0	0	0	0	0	0	0	.000
All-Star Game Totals			22	72	20	23	2	3	3	9	7	11	.319